The
Westminster
Standards

in Modern English

edited by

Kevin J. Bidwell

EP BOOKS
1st Floor Venture House, 6 Silver Court, Watchmead,
Welwyn Garden City, UK, AL7 1TS

www.epbooks.org
sales@epbooks.org

EP Books are distributed in the USA by:
JPL Distribution
3741 Linden Avenue Southeast
Grand Rapids, MI 49548

orders@jplbooks.com
www. jplbooks.com

British Library Cataloguing in Publication Data available

ISBN 978-1-78397-234-0

Printed and bound in Great Britain by Bell and Bain Ltd, Glasgow.

The Westminster Standards in Modern English Including the Creeds

Contents

The Westminster Confession of Faith in Modern English

Chapter 1

Of the Holy Scripture

1. Although the light of nature, and the works of creation and providence do so far manifest the goodness, wisdom, and power of God, as to leave men inexcusable;[1] yet are they not sufficient to give that knowledge of God, and of His will, which is necessary unto salvation.[2] Therefore it pleased the Lord, at sundry [various] times, and in divers manners [different ways], to reveal Himself, and to declare that His will unto His Church;[3] and afterwards for the better preserving and propagating of the truth, and for the more sure establishment and comfort of the Church against the corruption of the flesh, and the malice of Satan and of the world, to commit the same wholly unto writing;[4] which makes the Holy Scripture to be most necessary;[5] those former ways of God's revealing His will unto His people being now ceased.[6]

2. Under the name of Holy Scripture, or the Word of God written, are now contained all the books of the Old and New Testament, which are these:

Of the Old Testament:

Genesis, Exodus, Leviticus, Numbers, Deuteronomy, Joshua, Judges,

---

1   Romans 2:14-15; 1:19, 20; Psalm 19:1-3; Romans 1:32, 2:1.
2   1 Corinthians 1:21; 2:13-14
3   Hebrews 1:1
4   Proverbs 22:19-21; Luke 1:3-4; Romans 15:4; Matthew 4:4, 7, 10; Isaiah 8:19-20
5   2 Timothy 3:15; 2 Peter 1:19
6   Hebrews 1:1-2

Ruth, 1 Samuel, 11 Samuel, 1 Kings, 11 Kings, 1 Chronicles, 11 Chronicles, Ezra, Nehemiah, Esther, Job, Psalms, Proverbs, Ecclesiastes, The Song of Songs, Isaiah, Jeremiah, Lamentations, Ezekiel, Daniel, Hosea, Joel, Amos, Obadiah, Jonah, Micah, Nahum, Habakkuk, Zephaniah, Haggai, Zechariah, Malachi.

Of the New Testament:

The Gospels according to Matthew, Mark, Luke, John, The Acts of the Apostles, Paul's Epistles to the Romans, Corinthians 1, Corinthians 11, Galatians, Ephesians, Philippians, Colossians, Thessalonians 1, Thessalonians 11 , To Timothy 1, To Timothy 11, To Titus, To Philemon, The Epistle to the Hebrews, The Epistle of James, The first and second Epistles of Peter, The first, second, and third Epistles of John, The Epistle of Jude, The Revelation of John. All which are given by inspiration of God to be the rule of faith and life.[1]

3. The books commonly called Apocrypha, not being of divine inspiration, are no part of the canon of the Scripture, and therefore are of no authority in the Church of God, nor to be any otherwise approved, or made use of, than other human writings.[2]

4. The authority of the Holy Scripture, for which it ought to be believed and obeyed, depends not upon the testimony of any man, or Church; but wholly upon God (who is truth itself) the author thereof: and therefore it is to be received because it is the Word of God.[3]

5. We may be moved and induced [persuaded] by the testimony of the Church to a high and reverent esteem of the Holy Scripture.[4] And the heavenliness of the matter, the efficacy of the doctrine, the majesty of the style, the consent of all the parts, the scope of the whole (which is, to give all glory to God), the full discovery it makes of the only way of man's salvation, the many other incomparable excellencies, and the entire perfection thereof, are arguments whereby it does abundantly evidence itself to be the Word of God: yet notwithstanding, our full persuasion and assurance of the infallible truth and divine authority thereof, is from

---

1   Luke 16:29, 31; Ephesians 2:20; Revelation 22:18-19; 2 Timothy 3:16
2   Luke 24:27; Romans 3:2; 2 Peter 1:21
3   2 Peter 1:19, 21; 2 Timothy 3:16; 1 John 5:9; 1 Thessalonians 2:13
4   1 Timothy 3:15

the inward work of the Holy Spirit bearing witness by and with the Word in our hearts.[1]

6. The whole counsel of God concerning all things necessary for His own glory, man's salvation, faith and life, is either expressly set down in Scripture, or by good and necessary consequence may be deduced from Scripture: unto which nothing at any time is to be added, whether by new revelations of the Spirit, or traditions of men.[2] Nevertheless, we acknowledge the inward illumination of the Spirit of God to be necessary for the saving understanding of such things as are revealed in the Word:[3] and that there are some circumstances concerning the worship of God, and government of the Church, common to human actions and societies, which are to be ordered by the light of nature and Christian prudence, according to the general rules of the Word, which are always to be observed.[4]

7. All things in Scripture are not equally plain in themselves, nor equally clear unto all:[5] yet those things which are necessary to be known, believed, and observed for salvation are so clearly propounded, and opened in some place of Scripture or other, that not only the learned, but the unlearned, in a due use of the ordinary means, may attain unto a sufficient understanding of [learn to understand] them.[6]

8. The Old Testament in Hebrew (which was the native language of the people of God of old), and the New Testament in Greek (which, at the time of the writing of it, was most generally known to the nations), being immediately inspired by God, and, by His singular care and providence, kept pure in all ages, are therefore authentic;[7] so as, in all controversies of religion, the Church is finally to appeal unto them.[8] But, because these original tongues are not known to all the people of God, who have right unto, and interest in the Scriptures, and are commanded, in the fear of God, to read and search them,[9] therefore they are to be translated into the common language of every nation unto

---

1   1 John 2:20, 27; John 16:13- 14; 1 Corinthians 2:10-12; Isaiah 59:21
2   2 Timothy 3:15-17; Galatians 1:8-9; 2 Thessalonians 2:2
3   John 6:45; 1 Corinthians 2:9-12
4   1 Corinthians 11:13-14; 14:26, 40
5   2 Peter 3:16
6   Psalm 119:105, 130
7   Matthew 5:18
8   Isaiah 8:20; Acts 15:15; John 5:39, 46
9   John 5:39

which they come[1] that, the Word of God dwelling plentifully in all, they may worship Him in an acceptable manner;[2] and, through patience and comfort of the Scriptures, may have hope.[3]

9. The infallible rule of interpretation of Scripture is the Scripture itself: and therefore, when there is a question about the true and full sense of any Scripture (which is not manifold, but one), it must be searched and known by other places that speak more clearly.[4]

10. The supreme judge by which all controversies of religion are to be determined, and all decrees of councils, opinions of ancient writers, doctrines of men, and private spirits, are to be examined, and in whose sentence we are to rest, can be no other but the Holy Spirit speaking in the Scripture.[5]

Chapter 2
Of God, and of the Holy Trinity

1. There is but one only,[6] living, and true God,[7] who is infinite in being and perfection,[8] a most pure spirit,[9] invisible,[10] without body, parts,[11] or passions,[12] immutable,[13] immense,[14] eternal,[15] incomprehensible,[16] almighty,[17] most wise,[18] most holy,[19] most free,[20] most absolute;[21] working all things according to the counsel of His own immutable

---

1   1 Corinthians 14:6, 9, 11–12, 24, 27–28
2   Colossians 3:16
3   Romans 15:4
4   2 Peter 1:20–21; Acts 15:15–16
5   Matthew 22:29, 31; Ephesians 2:20; Acts 28:25
6   Deuteronomy 6:4; 1 Corinthians 8:4, 6
7   1 Thessalonians 1:9; Jeremiah 10:10
8   Job 11:7–9; 26:14
9   John 4:24
10   1 Timothy 1:17
11   Deuteronomy 4:15–16; John 4:24; Luke 24:39
12   Acts 14:11, 15
13   James 1:17; Malachi 3:6
14   1 Kings 8:27; Jeremiah 23:23–24
15   Psalm 90:2; 1 Timothy 1:17
16   Psalm 145:3
17   Genesis 17:1; Revelation 4:8
18   Romans 16:27
19   Isaiah 6:3; Revelation 4:8
20   Psalm 115:3
21   Exodus 3:14

and most righteous will,[1] for His own glory;[2] most loving,[3] gracious, merciful, long-suffering, abundant in goodness and truth, forgiving iniquity, transgression, and sin;[4] the rewarder of them that diligently seek Him;[5] and in addition, most just, and terrible in His judgments,[6] hating all sin,[7] and who will by no means clear the guilty.[8]

2. God has all life,[9] glory,[10] goodness,[11] blessedness,[12] in and of Himself; and is alone in and unto Himself all-sufficient, not standing in need of any creatures which He has made,[13] nor deriving any glory from them,[14] but only manifesting His own glory in, by, unto, and upon them: He is the alone fountain of all being, of whom, through whom, and to whom are all things;[15] and has most sovereign dominion over them, to do by them, for them, or upon them whatsoever Himself pleases.[16] In His sight all things are open and manifest;[17] His knowledge is infinite, infallible, and independent upon the creature,[18] so as nothing is to Him contingent [conditional], or uncertain.[19] He is most holy in all His counsels, in all His works, and in all His commands.[20] To Him is due from angels and men, and every other creature, whatsoever worship, service, or obedience He is pleased to require of them.[21]

3. In the unity of the Godhead there be three persons, of one substance, power, and eternity; God the Father, God the Son, and God the Holy Spirit.[22] The Father is of none, neither begotten nor

---

1 Ephesians 1:11
2 Proverbs 16:4; Romans 11:36
3 1 John 4:8, 16
4 Exodus 34:6–7
5 Hebrews 11:6
6 Nehemiah 9:32–33
7 Psalm 5:5–6
8 Nahum 1:2–3; Exodus 34:7
9 John 5:26
10 Acts 7:2
11 Psalm 119:68
12 1 Timothy 6:15; Romans 9:5
13 Acts 17:24–25
14 Job 22:2–3
15 Romans 11:36
16 Revelation 4:11; 1 Timothy 6:15; Daniel 4:25, 35
17 Hebrews 4:13
18 Romans 11:33–34; Psalm 147:5
19 Acts 15:18; Ezekiel 11:5
20 Psalm 145:17; Romans 7:12
21 Revelation 5:12–14
22 1 John 5:7; Matthew 3:16–17; Matthew 28:19; 2 Corinthians 13:14

proceeding; the Son is eternally begotten of the Father;[1] the Holy Spirit eternally proceeding from the Father and the Son.[2]

Chapter 3

Of God's Eternal Decree

1. God from all eternity, did, by the most wise and holy counsel of His own will, freely, and unchangeably ordain whatsoever comes to pass;[3] yet so, as thereby neither is God the author of sin,[4] nor is violence offered to the will of the creatures; nor is the liberty or contingency [possibility] of second causes taken away, but rather established.[5]

2. Although God knows whatsoever may or can come to pass upon all supposed conditions;[6] yet has He not decreed anything because He foresaw it as future, or as that which would come to pass upon such conditions.[7]

3. By the decree of God, for the manifestation of His glory, some men and angels[8] are predestined unto everlasting life; and others foreordained to everlasting death.[9]

4. These angels and men, thus predestined, and foreordained, are particularly and unchangeably designed, and their number so certain and definite, that it cannot be either increased or diminished.[10]

5. Those of mankind that are predestined unto life, God, before the foundation of the world was laid, according to His eternal and immutable purpose, and the secret counsel and good pleasure of His will, has chosen, in Christ, unto everlasting glory,[11] out of His mere free grace and love, without any foresight of faith, or good works, or perseverance in either of them, or any other thing in the creature, as

---

1   John 1:14, 18
2   John 15:26; Galatians 4:6
3   Ephesians 1:11; Romans 11:33; Hebrews 6:17; Romans 9:15, 18
4   James 1:13, 17; 1 John 1:5
5   Acts 2:23; Matthew 17:12; Acts 4:27–28; John 19:11; Proverbs 16:33
6   Acts 15:18; 1 Samuel 23:11–12; Matthew 11:21, 23
7   Romans 9:11, 13, 16, 18
8   1 Timothy 5:21; Matthew 25:41
9   Romans 9:22–23; Ephesians 1:5–6; Proverbs 16:4
10 2 Timothy 2:19; John 13:18
11 Ephesians 1:4, 9, 11; Romans 8:30; 2 Timothy 1:9; 1 Thessalonians 5:9

conditions, or causes moving Him thereunto:[1] and all to the praise of His glorious grace.[2]

6. As God has appointed the elect unto glory, so has He, by the eternal and most free purpose of His will, foreordained all the means thereunto.[2] Wherefore, they who are elected, being fallen in Adam, are redeemed by Christ,[4] are effectually called unto faith in Christ by His Spirit working in due season, are justified, adopted, sanctified,[5] and kept by His power, through faith, unto salvation.[6] Neither are any other redeemed by Christ, effectually called, justified, adopted, sanctified, and saved, but the elect only.[7]

7. The rest of mankind God was pleased, according to the unsearchable counsel of His own will, whereby He extends or withholds mercy, as He pleases, for the glory of His sovereign power over His creatures, to pass by; and to ordain them to dishonour and wrath, for their sin, to the praise of His glorious justice.[8]

8. The doctrine of this high mystery of predestination is to be handled with special prudence and care,[9] that men, attending the will of God revealed in His Word, and yielding obedience thereunto, may, from the certainty of their effectual calling, be assured of their eternal election.[10] So shall this doctrine afford matter of praise, reverence, and admiration of God;[11] and of humility, diligence, and abundant consolation to all that sincerely obey the Gospel.[12]

Chapter 4

Of Creation

1. It pleased God the Father, Son, and Holy Spirit,[13] for the

---

1   Romans 9:11, 13, 16; Ephesians 1:4, 9
2   Ephesians 1:6, 12
2   1 Peter 1:2; Ephesians 1:4–5; 2:10; 2 Thessalonians 2:13
4   1 Thessalonians 5:9–10; Titus 2:14
5   Romans 8:30; Ephesians 1:5; 2 Thessalonians 2:13
6   1 Peter 1:5
7   John 17:9; Romans 8:28–39; John 6:64–65; 10:26; 8:47; 1 John 2:19
8   Matthew 11:25–26; Romans 9:17–18, 21–22; 2 Timothy 2:19–20; Jude 4; 1 Peter 2:8
9   Romans 9:20; 11:33; Deuteronomy 29:29
10 2 Peter 1:10
11 Ephesians 1:6; Romans 11:33
12 Romans 11:5–6, 20; 2 Peter 1:10; Romans 8:33; Luke 10:20
13 Hebrews 1:2; John 1:2–3; Genesis 1:2; Job 26:13; 33:4

manifestation of the glory of His eternal power, wisdom, and goodness,[1] in the beginning, to create, or make of nothing, the world, and all things therein whether visible or invisible, in the space of six days; and all very good.[2]

2. After God had made all other creatures, He created man, male and female,[3] with reasonable and immortal souls,[4] endued with knowledge, righteousness, and true holiness, after His own image;[5] having the law of God written in their hearts,[6] and power to fulfil it;[7] and yet under a possibility of transgressing, being left to the liberty of their own will, which was subject unto change.[8] Beside this law written in their hearts, they received a command, not to eat of the tree of the knowledge of good and evil;[9] which while they kept, they were happy in their communion with God, and had dominion over the creatures.[10]

Chapter 5

Of Providence

1. God the great Creator of all things does uphold,[11] direct, dispose, and govern all creatures, actions, and things,[12] from the greatest even to the least,[13] by His most wise and holy providence,[14] according to His infallible foreknowledge,[15] and the free and immutable counsel of His own will,[16] to the praise of the glory of His wisdom, power, justice, goodness, and mercy.[17]

2. Although, in relation to the foreknowledge and decree of God,

1   Romans 1:20; Jeremiah 10:12; Psalm 104:24; 33:5–6
2   Genesis 1; Hebrews 11:3; Colossians 1:16; Acts 17:24
3   Genesis 1:27
4   Genesis 2:7; Ecclesiastes 12:7; Luke 23:43; Matthew 10:28
5   Genesis 1:26; Colossians 3:10; Ephesians 4:24
6   Romans 2:14–15
7   Ecclesiastes 7:29
8   Genesis 3:6; Ecclesiastes 7:29
9   Genesis 2:17, 3:8–11, 23
10 Genesis 1:26, 28
11 Hebrews 1:3
12 Daniel 4:34–35; Psalm 135:6; Acts 17:25–26, 28; Job 38–41
13 Matthew 10:29–31
14 Proverbs 15:3; Psalm 104:24; 145:17
15 Acts 15:18; Psalm 94:8–11
16 Ephesians 1:11; Psalm 33:10–11
17 Isaiah 63:14; Ephesians 3:10; Romans 9:17; Genesis 45:7; Psalm 145:7

the first Cause, all things come to pass immutably, and infallibly;[1] yet, by the same providence, He orders them to fall out, according to the nature of second causes, either necessarily, freely, or contingently [circumstantially].[2]

3. God, in His ordinary providence, makes use of means,[3] yet is free to work without,[4] above,[5] and against them,[6] at His pleasure.

4. The almighty power, unsearchable wisdom, and infinite goodness of God so far manifest themselves in His providence, that it extends itself even to the first fall, and all other sins of angels and men;[7] and that not by a bare [mere] permission,[8] but such as has joined with it a most wise and powerful bounding,[9] and otherwise ordering, and governing of them, in a manifold dispensation [varied administration], to His own holy ends;[10] yet so, as the sinfulness thereof proceeds only from the creature, and not from God, who, being most holy and righteous, neither is nor can be the author or approver of sin.[11]

5. The most wise, righteous, and gracious God does often leave, for a season, His own children to manifold temptations, and the corruption of their own hearts, to chastise them for their former sins, or to discover unto them the hidden strength of corruption and deceitfulness of their hearts, that they may be humbled;[12] and, to raise them to a more close and constant dependence for their support upon Himself, and to make them more watchful against all future occasions of sin, and for sundry other just and holy ends.[13]

6. As for those wicked and ungodly men whom God, as a righteous Judge, for former sins, does blind and harden,[14] from them He not only

---

1 Acts 2:23
2 Genesis 8:22; Jeremiah 31:35; Exodus 21:13; Deuteronomy 19:5; 1 Kings 22:28, 34; Isaiah 10:6–7
3 Acts 27:31, 44; Isaiah 55:10–11; Hosea 2:21–22
4 Hosea 1:7; Matthew 4:4; Job 34:10
5 Romans 4:19–21
6 2 Kings 6:6; Daniel 3:27
7 Romans 11:32–34; 2 Samuel 24:1; 1 Chronicles 21:1; 1 Kings 22:22–23; 1 Chronicles 10:4, 13–14; 2 Samuel 16:10; Acts 2:23; Acts 4:27–28
8 Acts 14:16
9 Psalm 76:10; 2 Kings 19:28
10 Genesis 50:20; Isaiah 10:6–7, 12
11 James 1:13–14, 17; 1 John 2:16; Psalm 50:21
12 2 Chronicles 32:25–26, 31; 2 Samuel 24:1
13 2 Corinthians 12:7–9; Psalm 73; 77:1–12; Mark 14:66–72; John 21:15–17
14 Romans 1:24, 26, 28; 11:7–8

withholds His grace whereby they might have been enlightened in their understandings, and wrought upon in their hearts;[1] but sometimes also withdraws the gifts which they had,[2] and exposes them to such objects as their corruption makes occasions of sin;[3] and, in addition, gives them over to their own lusts, the temptations of the world, and the power of Satan,[4] whereby it comes to pass that they harden themselves, even under those means which God uses for the softening of others.[5]

7. As the providence of God does, in general, reach to all creatures; so, after a most special manner, it takes care of His Church, and disposes all things to the good thereof.[6]

Chapter 6

Of the Fall of Man, of Sin, and the Punishment thereof

1. Our first parents, being seduced by the subtlety and temptations of Satan, sinned, in eating the forbidden fruit.[7] This their sin, God was pleased, according to His wise and holy counsel, to permit, having purposed to order it to His own glory.[8]

2. By this sin they fell from their original righteousness and communion with God,[9] and so became dead in sin,[10] and wholly defiled in all the faculties and parts of soul and body.[11]

3. They being the root of all mankind, the guilt of this sin was imputed;[12] and the same death in sin, and corrupted nature, conveyed to all their posterity descending from them by ordinary generation.[13]

4. From this original corruption, whereby we are utterly indisposed,

---

1   Deuteronomy 29:4
2   Matthew 13:12; 25:29
3   Deuteronomy 2:30; 2 Kings 8:12–13
4   Psalm 81:11–12; 2 Thessalonians 2:10–12
5   Exodus 7:3; 8:15, 32; 2 Corinthians 2:15, 16; Isaiah 8:14; 1 Peter 2:7–8; Isaiah 6:9–10; Acts 28:26–27
6   1 Timothy 4:10; Amos 9:8–9; Romans 8:28; Isaiah 43:3–5, 14
7   Genesis 3:13; 2 Corinthians 11:3
8   Romans 11:32
9   Genesis 3:6–8; Ecclesiastes 7:29; Romans 3:23
10   Genesis 2:17; Ephesians 2:1
11   Titus 1:15; Genesis 6:5; Jeremiah 17:9; Romans 3:10–18
12   Genesis 1:27–28; 2:16–17; Acts 17:26; Romans 5:12, 15–19; 1 Corinthians 15:21–22, 49
13   Psalm 51:5; Genesis 5:3; Job 14:4; 15:14

disabled, and made opposite to all good,[1] and wholly inclined to all evil,[2] do proceed all actual transgressions.[3]

5. This corruption of nature, during this life, does remain in those that are regenerated;[4] and although it be, through Christ, pardoned, and mortified; yet both itself, and all the motions thereof, are truly and properly sin.[5]

6. Every sin, both original and actual, being a transgression of the righteous law of God, and contrary thereunto,[6] does in its own nature, bring guilt upon the sinner,[7] whereby he is bound over to the wrath of God,[8] and curse of the law,[9] and so made subject to death,[10] with all miseries spiritual,[11] temporal,[12] and eternal.[13]

Chapter 7
Of God's Covenant with Man

1. The distance between God and the creature is so great, that although reasonable creatures do owe obedience unto Him as their Creator, yet they could never have any fruition [enjoyment] of Him as their blessedness and reward, but by some voluntary condescension on God's part, which He has been pleased to express by way of covenant.[14]

2. The first covenant made with man was a covenant of works,[15] wherein life was promised to Adam, and in him to his posterity,[16] upon condition of perfect and personal obedience.[17]

---

1   Romans 5:6, 8:7; 7:18; Colossians 1:21
2   Genesis 6:5; 8:21; Romans 3:10-12
3   James 1:14-15; Ephesians 2:2-3; Matthew 15:19
4   1 John 1:8, 10; Romans 7:14, 17-18, 23; James 3:2; Proverbs 20:9; Ecclesiastes 7:20
5   Romans 7:5, 7-8, 25; Galatians 5:17
6   1 John 3:4
7   Romans 2:15, 3:9, 19
8   Ephesians 2:3
9   Galatians 3:10
10 Romans 6:23
11 Ephesians 4:18
12 Romans 8:20; Lamentations 3:39
13 Matthew 25:41; 2 Thessalonians 1:9
14 Isaiah 40:13-17; Job 9:32, 33; 1 Samuel 2:25; Psalm 113:5-6, 100:2-3; Job 22:2-3; 35:7-8; Luke 17:10; Acts 17:24-25
15 Galatians 3:12
16 Romans 10:5; Romans 5:12-20
17 Genesis 2:17; Galatians 3:10

3. Man, by his fall, having made himself incapable of life by that covenant, the Lord was pleased to make a second,[1] commonly called the covenant of grace; wherein He freely offers unto sinners life and salvation by Jesus Christ; requiring of them faith in Him, that they may be saved,[2] and promising to give unto all those that are ordained unto life His Holy Spirit, to make them willing, and able to believe.[3]

4. This covenant of grace is frequently set forth in Scripture by the name of a Testament, in reference to the death of Jesus Christ the Testator, and to the everlasting inheritance, with all things belonging to it, therein bequeathed.[4]

5. This covenant was differently administered in the time of the law, and in the time of the gospel:[5] under the law, it was administered by promises, prophecies, sacrifices, circumcision, the paschal [Passover] lamb, and other types and ordinances delivered to the people of the Jews, all foreshadowing Christ to come;[6] which were, for that time, sufficient and efficacious, through the operation of the Spirit, to instruct and build up the elect in faith in the promised Messiah,[7] by whom they had full remission of sins, and eternal salvation; and is called the Old Testament.[8]

6. Under the gospel, when Christ, the substance,[9] was exhibited, the ordinances in which this covenant is dispensed are the preaching of the Word, and the administration of the sacraments of Baptism and the Lord's Supper:[10] which, though fewer in number, and administered with more simplicity, and less outward glory; yet, in them, it is held forth in more fullness, evidence, and spiritual efficacy,[11] to all nations, both Jews and Gentiles;[12] and is called the New Testament.[13] There are not therefore

---

1   Galatians 3:21; Romans 8:3; 3:20–21; Genesis 3:15; Isaiah 42:6
2   Mark 16:15–16; John 3:16; Romans 10:6, 9; Galatians 3:11
3   Ezekiel 36:26–27; John 6:44–45
4   Hebrews 9:15–17; 7:22; Luke 22:20; 1 Corinthians 11:25
5   2 Corinthians 3:6–9
6   Hebrews 8, 9, and 10; Romans 4:11; Colossians 2:11–12; 1 Corinthians 5:7
7   1 Corinthians 10:1–4; Hebrews 11:13; John 8:56
8   Galatians 3:7–9, 14
9   Colossians 2:17
10   Matthew 28:19–20; 1 Corinthians 11:23–25
11   Hebrews 12:22–28; Jeremiah 31:33–34
12   Matthew 28:19; Ephesians 2:15–19
13   Luke 22:20

two covenants of grace, differing in substance, but one and the same, under various dispensations [administrations].[1]

Chapter 8

Of Christ the Mediator

1. It pleased God, in His eternal purpose, to choose and ordain the Lord Jesus, His only begotten Son, to be the Mediator between God and man,[2] the Prophet,[3] Priest,[4] and King,[5] the Head and Saviour of His Church,[6] the Heir of all things,[7] and Judge of the world:[8] unto whom He did from all eternity give a people, to be His seed,[9] and to be by Him in time redeemed, called, justified, sanctified, and glorified.[10]

2. The Son of God, the second person of the Trinity, being very and eternal God, of one substance and equal with the Father, did, when the fullness of time was come, take upon Him man's nature,[11] with all the essential properties, and common infirmities thereof, yet without sin;[12] being conceived by the power of the Holy Spirit, in the womb of the virgin Mary, of her substance.[13] So that two whole, perfect, and distinct natures, the Godhead and the manhood, were inseparably joined together in one person, without conversion, composition, or confusion.[14] Which person is very God, and very man, yet one Christ, the only Mediator between God and man.[15]

3. The Lord Jesus, in His human nature thus united to the divine, was sanctified, and anointed with the Holy Spirit, above measure,[16]

---

1 Galatians 3:14, 16; Romans 3:21–23, 30; Psalm 32:1 with Romans 4:3, 6, 16–17, 23–24; Hebrews 13:8; Acts 15:11
2 Isaiah 42:1; 1 Peter 1:19–20; John 3:16; 1 Timothy 2:5
3 Acts 3:22
4 Hebrews 5:5–6
5 Psalm 2:6; Luke 1:33
6 Ephesians 5:23
7 Hebrews 1:2
8 Acts 17:31
9 John 17:6; Psalm 22:30; Isaiah 53:10
10 1 Timothy 2:6; Isaiah 55:4–5; 1 Corinthians 1:30
11 John 1:1, 14; 1 John 5:20; Philippians 2:6; Galatians 4:4
12 Hebrews 2:14, 16–17; 4:15
13 Luke 1:27, 31, 35; Galatians 4:4
14 Luke 1:35; Colossians 2:9; Romans 9:5; 1 Peter 3:18; 1 Timothy 3:16
15 Romans 1:3–4; 1 Timothy 2:5
16 Psalm 45:7; John 3:34

having in Him all the treasures of wisdom and knowledge;[1] in whom it pleased the Father that all fullness should dwell;[2] to the end that, being holy, harmless, undefiled, and full of grace and truth,[3] He might be thoroughly furnished to execute the office of a Mediator and Surety.[4] Which office He took not unto Himself, but was thereunto called by His Father,[5] who put all power and judgment into His hand, and gave Him commandment to execute the same.[6]

4. This office the Lord Jesus did most willingly undertake;[7] which that He might discharge, He was made under the law,[8] and did perfectly fulfil it;[9] endured most grievous torments immediately in His soul,[10] and most painful sufferings in His body;[11] was crucified, and died;[12] was buried, and remained under the power of death; yet saw no corruption.[13] On the third day He arose from the dead,[14] with the same body in which He suffered,[15] with which also he ascended into heaven, and there sits at the right hand of His Father,[16] making intercession,[17] and shall return, to judge men and angels, at the end of the world.[18]

5. The Lord Jesus, by His perfect obedience, and sacrifice of Himself, which He through the eternal Spirit, once offered up unto God, has fully satisfied the justice of His Father;[19] and purchased, not only reconciliation, but an everlasting inheritance in the kingdom of heaven, for all those whom the Father has given unto Him.[20]

6. Although the work of redemption was not actually wrought by Christ

---

1   Colossians 2:3
2   Colossians 1:19
3   Hebrews 7:26; John 1:14
4   Acts 10:38; Hebrews 12:24; 7:22
5   Hebrews 5:4-5
6   John 5:22, 27; Matthew 28:18; Acts 2:36
7   Psalm 40:7-8; Hebrews 10:5-10; John 10:18; Philippians 2:8
8   Galatians 4:4
9   Matthew 3:15; 5:17
10 Matthew26:37-38; Luke 22:44; Matthew 27:46
11 Matthew 26 and 27
12 Philippians 2:8
13 Acts 2:23-24, 27; Acts 13:37; Romans 6:9
14 1 Corinthians 15:3-4
15 John 20:25, 27
16 Mark 16:19
17 Romans 8:34; Hebrews 9:24; 7:25
18 Romans 14:9-10; Acts 1:11; 10:42; Matthew 13:40-42; Jude 6; 2 Peter 2:4
19 Romans 5:19; Hebrews 9:14, 16; 10:14; Ephesians 5:2; Romans 3:25-26
20 Daniel 9:24, 26; Colossians 1:19-20; Ephesians 1:11, 14; John 17:2; Hebrews 9:12, 15

till after His incarnation, yet the virtue, efficacy, and benefits thereof were communicated unto the elect, in all ages successively from the beginning of the world, in and by those promises, types, and sacrifices, wherein He was revealed, and signified to be the seed of the woman which should bruise the serpent's head; and the Lamb slain from the beginning of the world; being yesterday and today the same, and forever.[1]

7. Christ, in the work of mediation, acts according to both natures, by each nature doing that which is proper to itself;[2] yet, by reason of the unity of the person, that which is proper to one nature is sometimes in Scripture attributed to the person denominated by the other nature.[3]

8. To all those for whom Christ has purchased redemption, He does certainly and effectually apply and communicate the same,[4] making intercession for them,[5] and revealing unto them, in and by the Word, the mysteries of salvation;[6] effectually persuading them by His Spirit to believe and obey, and governing their hearts by His Word and Spirit;[7] overcoming all their enemies by His almighty power and wisdom, in such manner, and ways, as are most consonant [agreeable] to His wonderful and unsearchable dispensation [administration].[8]

Chapter 9

Of Free Will

1. God has endued the will of man with that natural liberty, that it is neither forced, nor, by any absolute necessity of nature, determined to good, or evil.[9]

2. Man, in his state of innocence, had freedom, and power to will and to do that which was good and well pleasing to God;[10] but yet, mutably [able to change], so that he might fall from it.[11]

---

1 Galatians 4:4–5; Genesis 3:15; Revelation 13:8; Hebrews 13:8
2 Hebrews 9:14; 1 Peter 3:18
3 Acts 20:28; John 3:13; 1 John 3:16
4 John 6:37, 39; John 10:15–16
5 1 John 2:1–2; Romans 8:34
6 John 15:13, 15; Ephesians 1:7–9; John 17:6
7 John 14:26; Hebrews 12:2; 2 Corinthians 4:13; Romans 8:9, 14; 15:18–19; John 17:17
8 Psalm 110:1; 1 Corinthians 15:25–26; Malachi 4:2–3; Colossians 2:15
9 Matthew 17:12; James 1:14; Deuteronomy 30:19
10 Ecclesiastes 7:29; Genesis 1:26
11 Genesis 2:16–17; 3:6

3. Man, by his fall into a state of sin, has wholly lost all ability of will to any spiritual good accompanying salvation:[1] so as, a natural man, being altogether averse from that good,[2] and dead in sin,[3] is not able, by his own strength, to convert himself, or to prepare himself thereunto.[4]

4. When God converts a sinner, and translates him into the state of grace, He frees him from his natural bondage under sin;[5] and, by His grace alone, enables him freely to will and to do that which is spiritually good;[6] yet so, as that by reason of his remaining corruption, he does not perfectly, nor only, will that which is good, but does also will that which is evil.[7]

5. The will of man is made perfectly and immutably free to do good alone in the state of glory only.[8]

Chapter 10

Of Effectual Calling

1. All those whom God has predestined unto life, and those only, He is pleased, in His appointed time, effectually to call,[9] by His Word and Spirit,[10] out of that state of sin and death, in which they are by nature, to grace and salvation, by Jesus Christ;[11] enlightening their minds spiritually and savingly to understand the things of God,[12] taking away their heart of stone, and giving unto them a heart of flesh;[13] renewing their wills, and, by His almighty power, determining them to that which is good,[14] and effectually drawing them to Jesus Christ:[15] yet so, as they come most freely, being made willing by His grace.[16]

---

1   Romans 5:6; 8:7; John 15:5
2   Romans 3:10, 12
3   Ephesians 2:1, 5; Colossians 2:13
4   John 6:44, 65; Ephesians 2:2–5; 1 Corinthians 2:14; Titus 3:3–5
5   Colossians 1:13; John 8:34, 36
6   Philippians 2:13; Romans 6:18, 22
7   Galatians 5:17; Romans 7:15, 18–19, 21, 23
8   Ephesians 4:13; Hebrews 12:23; 1 John 3:2; Jude 24
9   Romans 8:30; 11:7; Ephesians 1:10–11
10 2 Thessalonians 2:13–14; 2 Corinthians 3:3, 6
11 Romans 8:2; Ephesians 2:1–5; 2 Timothy 1:9–10
12 Acts 26:18; 1 Corinthians 2:10, 12; Ephesians 1:17–18
13 Ezekiel 36:26
14 Ezekiel 11:19; Philippians 2:13; Deuteronomy 30:6; Ezekiel 36:27
15 Ephesians 1:19; John 6:44–45
16 Song of Solomon 1:4; Psalm 110:3; John 6:37; Romans 6:16–18

2. This effectual call is of God's free and special grace alone, not from anything at all foreseen in man,[1] who is altogether passive therein, until, being quickened and renewed by the Holy Spirit,[2] he is thereby enabled to answer this call, and to embrace the grace offered and conveyed in it.[3]

3. Elect infants, dying in infancy, are regenerated, and saved by Christ, through the Spirit,[4] who works when, and where, and how He pleases:[5] so also are all other elect persons who are incapable of being outwardly called by the ministry of the Word.[6]

4. Others, not elected, although they may be called by the ministry of the Word,[7] and may have some common operations of the Spirit,[8] yet they never truly come unto Christ, and therefore cannot be saved:[9] much less can men, not professing the Christian religion, be saved in any other way whatsoever, be they never so diligent to frame their lives according to the light of nature, and the laws of that religion they do profess.[10] And to assert and maintain that they may, is very pernicious, and to be detested.[11]

Chapter 11

Of Justification

1. Those whom God effectually calls, He also freely justifies;[12] not by infusing righteousness into them, but by pardoning their sins, and by accounting and accepting their persons as righteous; not for anything wrought in them, or done by them, but for Christ's sake alone; nor by imputing faith itself, the act of believing, or any other evangelical obedience to them, as their righteousness; but by imputing

---

1 2 Timothy 1:9; Titus 3:4-5; Ephesians 2:4-5, 8-9; Romans 9:11
2 1 Corinthians 2:14; Romans 8:7; Ephesians 2:5
3 John 6:37; Ezekiel 36:27; John 5:25
4 Luke 18:15-16 and Acts 2:38-39 and John 3:3, 5 and 1 John 5:12 and Romans 8:9 [compared together]
5 John 3:8
6 1 John 5:12; Acts 4:12
7 Matthew 22:14
8 Matthew 7:22; 13:20-21; Hebrews 6:4-5
9 John 6:64-66; 8:24
10 Acts 4:12; John 14:6; Ephesians 2:12; John 4:22; 17:3
11 2 John 9-11; 1 Corinthians 16:22; Galatians 1:6-8
12 Romans 8:30; 3:24

the obedience and satisfaction of Christ unto them,[1] they receiving and resting on Him and His righteousness, by faith; which faith they have not of themselves, it is the gift of God.[2]

2. Faith, thus receiving and resting on Christ and His righteousness, is the alone instrument of justification:[3] yet is it not alone in the person justified, but is ever accompanied with all other saving graces, and is no dead faith, but works by love.[4]

3. Christ, by His obedience and death, did fully discharge the debt of all those that are thus justified, and did make a proper, real and full satisfaction to His Father's justice in their behalf.[5] Yet, in as much as He was given by the Father for them;[6] and His obedience and satisfaction accepted in their stead;[7] and both, freely, not for anything in them; their justification is only of free grace;[8] that both the exact justice, and rich grace of God might be glorified in the justification of sinners.[9]

4. God did, from all eternity, decree to justify all the elect,[10] and Christ did, in the fullness of time, die for their sins, and rise again for their justification:[11] nevertheless, they are not justified, until the Holy Spirit does, in due time, actually apply Christ unto them.[12]

5. God does continue to forgive the sins of those that are justified;[13] and although they can never fall from the state of justification,[14] yet they may, by their sins, fall under God's fatherly displeasure, and not have the light of His countenance restored unto them, until they humble themselves, confess their sins, beg pardon, and renew their faith and repentance.[15]

6. The justification of believers under the Old Testament was, in all

---

1 Romans 4:5–8; 2 Corinthians 5:19, 21; Romans 3:22, 24–25, 27–28; Titus 3:5, 7; Ephesians 1:7; Jeremiah 23:6; 1 Corinthians 1:30–31; Romans 5:17–19
2 Acts 10:43; Galatians 2:16; Philippians 3:9; Acts 13:38–39; Ephesians 2:7–8
3 John 1:12; Romans 3:28; 5:1
4 James 2:17, 22, 26; Galatians 5:6
5 Romans 5:8–10, 19; 1 Timothy 2:5–6; Hebrews 10:10, 14; Daniel 9:24, 26; Isaiah 53:4–6, 10–12
6 Romans 8:32
7 2 Corinthians 5:21; Matthew 3:17; Ephesians 5:2
8 Romans 3:24; Ephesians 1:7
9 Romans 3:26; Ephesians 2:7
10 Galatians 3:8; 1 Peter 1:2, 19–20; Romans 8:30
11 Galatians 4:4; 1 Timothy 2:6; Romans 4:25
12 Colossians 1:21–22; Galatians 2:16; Titus 3:3–7
13 Matthew 6:12; 1 John 1:7, 9; 1 John 2:1–2
14 Luke 22:32; John 10:28; Hebrews 10:14
15 Psalm 89:31–33; 51:7–12; 32:5; Matthew 26:75; 1 Corinthians 11:30; Luke 1:20

these respects, one and the same with the justification of believers under the New Testament.[1]

Chapter 12

Of Adoption

1. All those that are justified, God vouchsafes [promises], in and for His only Son Jesus Christ, to make partakers of the grace of adoption,[2] by which they are taken into the number, and enjoy the liberties and privileges of the children of God,[3] have His name put upon them,[4] receive the spirit of adoption,[5] have access to the throne of grace with boldness,[6] are enabled to cry, Abba, Father,[7] are pitied,[8] protected,[9] provided for,[10] and chastened by Him as by a Father:[11] yet never cast off,[12] but sealed to the day of redemption;[13] and inherit the promises,[14] as heirs of everlasting salvation.[15]

Chapter 13

Of Sanctification

1. They, who are once effectually called, and regenerated, having a new heart, and a new spirit created in them, are further sanctified, really and personally, through the virtue of Christ's death and resurrection,[16] by His Word and Spirit dwelling in them:[17] the dominion of the whole body of sin is destroyed,[18] and the several lusts thereof are more and

---

1   Galatians 3:9, 13–14; Romans 4:22–24; Hebrews 13:8
2   Ephesians 1:5
3   Galatians 4:4–5; Romans 8:17; John 1:12
4   Jeremiah 14:9; 2 Corinthians 6:18; Revelation 3:12
5   Romans 8:15
6   Ephesians 3:12; Romans 5:2
7   Galatians 4:6
8   Psalm 103:13
9   Proverbs 14:26
10 Matthew 6:30, 32; 1 Peter 5:7
11 Hebrews 12:6
12 Lamentations 3:31
13 Ephesians 4:30
14 Hebrews 6:12
15 1 Peter 1:3–4; Hebrews 1:14
16 1 Corinthians 6:11; Acts 20:32; Philippians 3:10; Romans 6:5–6
17 John 17:17; Ephesians 5:26; 2 Thessalonians 2:13
18 Romans 6:6, 14

more weakened and mortified;[1] and they more and more quickened and strengthened in all saving graces,[2] to the practice of true holiness, without which no man shall see the Lord.[3]

2. This sanctification is throughout, in the whole man;[4] yet imperfect in this life, there abiding still some remnants of corruption in every part;[5] whence arises a continual and irreconcilable war, the flesh lusting against the Spirit, and the Spirit against the flesh.[6]

3. In which war, although the remaining corruption, for a time, may much prevail;[7] yet, through the continual supply of strength from the sanctifying Spirit of Christ, the regenerate part does overcome;[8] and so, the saints grow in grace,[9] perfecting holiness in the fear of God.[10]

Chapter 14

Of Saving Faith

1. The grace of faith, whereby the elect are enabled to believe to the saving of their souls,[11] is the work of the Spirit of Christ in their hearts,[12] and is ordinarily wrought by the ministry of the Word:[13] by which also, and by the administration of the sacraments, and prayer, it is increased and strengthened.[14]

2. By this faith, a Christian believes to be true whatsoever is revealed in the Word, for the authority of God Himself speaking therein;[15] and acts differently upon that which each particular passage thereof contains; yielding obedience to the commands,[16] trembling at the threatenings,[17]

---

1 Galatians 5:24; Romans 8:13
2 Colossians 1:11; Ephesians 3:16–19
3 2 Corinthians 7:1; Hebrews 12:14
4 1 Thessalonians 5:23
5 1 John 1:10; Romans 7:18, 23; Philippians 3:12
6 Galatians 5:17; 1 Peter 2:11
7 Romans 7:23
8 Romans 6:14; 1 John 5:4; Ephesians 4:15–16
9 2 Peter 3:18; 2 Corinthians 3:18
10 2 Corinthians 7:1
11 Hebrews 10:39
12 2 Corinthians 4:13; Ephesians 1:17–19; Ephesians 2:8
13 Romans 10:14, 17
14 1 Peter 2:2; Acts 20:32; Romans 4:11; Luke 17:5; Romans 1:16–17
15 John 4:42; 1 Thessalonians 2:13; 1 John 5:10; Acts 24:14
16 Romans 16:26
17 Isaiah 66:2

and embracing the promises of God for this life, and that which is to come.[1] But the principal acts of saving faith are accepting, receiving, and resting upon Christ alone for justification, sanctification, and eternal life, by virtue of the covenant of grace.[2]

3. This faith is different in degrees, weak or strong;[3] may be often and many ways assailed, and weakened, but gets the victory;[4] growing up in many to the attainment of a full assurance, through Christ,[5] who is both the author and finisher of our faith.[6]

Chapter 15

Of Repentance unto Life

1. Repentance unto life is an evangelical grace,[7] the doctrine whereof is to be preached by every minister of the Gospel, as well as that of faith in Christ.[8]

2. By it, a sinner, out of the sight and sense not only of the danger, but also of the filthiness and odiousness of his sins, as contrary to the holy nature, and righteous law of God; and upon the apprehension of His mercy in Christ to such as are penitent, so grieves for, and hates his sins, as to turn from them all unto God,[9] purposing and endeavouring to walk with Him in all the ways of His commandments.[10]

3. Although repentance is not to be rested in, as any satisfaction for sin, or any cause of the pardon thereof,[11] which is the act of God's free grace in Christ,[12] yet it is of such necessity to all sinners, that none may expect pardon without it.[13]

---

1   Hebrews 11:13; 1 Timothy 4:8
2   John 1:12; Acts 16:31; Galatians 2:20; Acts 15:11
3   Hebrews 5:13-14; Romans 4:19-20; Matthew 6:30; Matthew 8:10
4   Luke 22:31-32; Ephesians 6:16; 1 John 5:4-5
5   Hebrews 6:11-12; 10:22; Colossians 2:2
6   Hebrews 12:2
7   Zechariah 12:10; Acts 11:18
8   Luke 24:47; Mark 1:15; Acts 20:21
9   Ezekiel 18:30-31; 36:31; Isaiah 30:22; Psalm 51:4; Jeremiah 31:18-19; Joel 2:12-13; Amos 5:15; Psalm 119:128; 2 Corinthians 7:11
10 Psalm 119:6, 59, 106; Luke 1:6; 2 Kings 23:25
11 Ezekiel 36:31-32; 16:61-63
12 Hosea 14:2, 4; Romans 3:24; Ephesians 1:7
13 Luke 13:3, 5; Acts 17:30-31

4. As there is no sin so small, but it deserves damnation;[1] so there is no sin so great, that it can bring damnation upon those who truly repent.[2]

5. Men ought not to content themselves with a general repentance, but it is every man's duty to endeavour to repent of his particular sins, particularly.[3]

6. As every man is bound to make private confession of his sins to God, praying for the pardon thereof;[4] upon which, and the forsaking of them, he shall find mercy;[5] so he that scandalizes his brother, or the Church of Christ, ought to be willing, by a private or public confession and sorrow for his sin, to declare his repentance to those that are offended,[6] who are thereupon to be reconciled to him, and in love to receive him.[7]

Chapter 16

Of Good Works

1. Good works are only such as God has commanded in His holy Word,[8] and not such as, without the warrant thereof, are devised by men, out of blind zeal, or upon any pretence of good intention.[9]

2. These good works, done in obedience to God's commandments, are the fruits and evidences of a true and lively faith:[10] and by them believers manifest their thankfulness,[11] strengthen their assurance,[12] edify their brethren,[13] adorn the profession of the Gospel,[14] stop the mouths of the adversaries,[15] and glorify God,[16] whose workmanship they are, created in

---

1   Romans 6:23; 5:12; Matthew 12:36
2   Isaiah 55:7; Romans 8:1; Isaiah 1:16, 18
3   Psalm 19:13; Luke 19:8; 1 Timothy 1:13, 15
4   Psalm 51:4–5, 7, 9, 14; 32:5–6
5   Proverbs 28:13; 1 John 1:9
6   James 5:16; Luke 17:3–4; Joshua 7:19; Psalm 51
7   2 Corinthians 2:8
8   Micah 6:8; Romans 12:2; Hebrews 13:21
9   Matthew 15:9; Isaiah 29:13; 1 Peter 1:18; Romans 10:2; John 16:2; 1 Samuel 15:21–23
10 James 2:18, 22
11 Psalm 116:12–13; 1 Peter 2:9
12 1 John 2:3, 5; 2 Peter 1:5–10
13 2 Corinthians 9:2; Matthew 5:16
14 Titus 2:5, 9–12; 1 Timothy 6:1
15 1 Peter 2:15
16 1 Peter 2:12; Philippians 1:11; John 15:8

Christ Jesus thereunto,[1] that, having their fruit unto holiness, they may have the end, eternal life.[2]

3. Their ability to do good works is not at all of themselves, but wholly from the Spirit of Christ.[3] And that they may be enabled thereunto, beside the graces they have already received, there is required an actual influence of the same Holy Spirit, to work in them to will, and to do, of His good pleasure:[4] yet are they not hereupon to grow negligent, as if they were not bound to perform any duty unless upon a special motion of the Spirit; but they ought to be diligent in stirring up the grace of God that is in them.[5]

4. They who, in their obedience, attain to the greatest height which is possible in this life, are so far from being able to supererogate [go beyond duty], and to do more than God requires, as that they fall short of much which in duty they are bound to do.[6]

5. We cannot by our best works merit pardon of sin, or eternal life at the hand of God, by reason of the great disproportion that is between them and the glory to come; and the infinite distance that is between us and God, whom, by them, we can neither profit, nor satisfy for the debt of our former sins,[7] but when we have done all we can, we have done but our duty, and are unprofitable servants:[8] and because, as they are good, they proceed from His Spirit,[9] and as they are wrought by us, they are defiled, and mixed with so much weakness and imperfection, that they cannot endure the severity of God's judgment.[10]

6. Notwithstanding, the persons of believers being accepted through Christ, their good works also are accepted in Him;[11] not as though they were in this life wholly un-blameable and un-reproveable in God's

---

1   Ephesians 2:10
2   Romans 6:22
3   John 15:4–5; Ezekiel 36:26–27
4   Philippians 2:13; 4:13; 2 Corinthians 3:5
5   Philippians 2:12; Hebrews 6:11–12; 2 Peter 1:3, 5, 10–11; Isaiah 64:7; 2 Timothy 1:6; Acts 26:6–7; Jude 20–21
6   Luke 17:10; Nehemiah 13:22; Job 9:2–3; Galatians 5:17
7   Romans 3:20; 4:2, 4, 6; Ephesians 2:8–9; Titus 3:5–7; Romans 8:18; Psalm 16:2; Job 22:2–3; Job 35:7–8
8   Luke 17:10
9   Galatians 5:22–23
10 Isaiah 64:6; Galatians 5:17; Romans 7:15, 18; Psalm 143:2; 130:3
11 Ephesians 1:6; 1 Peter 2:5; Exodus 28:38; Genesis 4:4; Hebrews 11:4

sight;[1] but that He, looking upon them in His Son, is pleased to accept and reward that which is sincere, although accompanied with many weaknesses and imperfections.[2]

7. Works done by unregenerate men, although for the matter of them they may be things which God commands; and of good use both to themselves and others:[3] yet, because they proceed not from an heart purified by faith;[4] nor are done in a right manner, according to the Word;[5] nor to a right end, the glory of God;[6] they are therefore sinful and cannot please God, or make a man meet to receive grace from God:[7] and yet, their neglect of them is more sinful and displeasing unto God.[8]

Chapter 17

Of the Perseverance of the Saints

1. They, whom God has accepted in His Beloved, effectually called, and sanctified by His Spirit, can neither totally nor finally fall away from the state of grace: but shall certainly persevere therein to the end, and be eternally saved.[9]

2. This perseverance of the saints depends not upon their own free will, but upon the immutability of the decree of election, flowing from the free and unchangeable love of God the Father;[10] upon the efficacy of the merit and intercession of Jesus Christ,[11] the abiding of the Spirit, and of the seed of God within them,[12] and the nature of the covenant of grace:[13] from all which arises also the certainty and infallibility thereof.[14]

3. Nevertheless, they may, through the temptations of Satan and of the world, the prevalence of corruption remaining in them, and the

---

1 Job 9:20; Psalm 143:2
2 Hebrews 13:20-21; 2 Corinthians 8:12; Hebrews 6:10; Matthew 25:21, 23
3 2 Kings 10:30-31; 1 Kings 21:27, 29; Philippians 1:15-16. 18
4 Genesis 4:5 with Hebrews 11:4; Hebrews 11:6
5 1 Corinthians 13:3; Isaiah 1:12
6 Matthew 6:2, 5, 16
7 Haggai 2:14; Titus 1:15; Amos 5:21-22; Hosea 1:4; Romans 9:16; Titus 3:5
8 Psalm 14:4; 36:3; Job 21:14-15; Matthew 25:41-43, 45; 23:23
9 Philippians 1:6; 2 Peter 1:10; John 10:28-29; 3:9; 1 Peter 1:5, 9
10 2 Timothy 2:18-19; Jeremiah 31:3
11 Hebrews 10:10, 14; 13:20-21; 9:12-15; Romans 8:33-39; John 17:11, 24; Luke 22:32; Hebrews 7:25
12 John 14:16-17; 1 John 2:27; 1 John 3:9
13 Jeremiah 32:40
14 John 10:28; 2 Thessalonians 3:3; 1 John 2:19

neglect of the means of their preservation, fall into grievous sins;[1] and, for a time, continue therein:[2] whereby they incur God's displeasure,[3] and grieve His Holy Spirit,[4] come to be deprived of some measure of their graces and comforts,[5] have their hearts hardened,[6] and their consciences wounded;[7] hurt and scandalize others,[8] and bring temporal judgments upon themselves.[9]

Chapter 18
Of Assurance of Grace and Salvation

1. Although hypocrites and other unregenerate men may vainly deceive themselves with false hopes and carnal presumptions of being in the favour of God, and estate of salvation[10] (which hope of theirs shall perish):[11] yet such as truly believe in the Lord Jesus, and love Him in sincerity, endeavouring to walk in all good conscience before Him, may, in this life, be certainly assured that they are in the state of grace,[12] and may rejoice in the hope of the glory of God, which hope shall never make them ashamed.[13]

2. This certainty is not a bare conjectural and probable persuasion grounded upon a fallible hope;[14] but an infallible assurance of faith founded upon the divine truth of the promises of salvation,[15] the inward evidence of those graces unto which these promises are made,[16] the testimony of the Spirit of adoption witnessing with our spirits that we

---

1   Matthew 26:70, 72, 74
2   Psalm 51 [title], 14
3   Isaiah 64:5, 7, 9; 2 Samuel 11:27
4   Ephesians 4:30
5   Psalm 51:8, 10, 12; Revelation 2:4; Song of Solomon 5:2–4, 6
6   Isaiah 63:17; Mark 6:52; 16:14
7   Psalm 32:3–4; 51:8
8   2 Samuel 12:14
9   Psalm 89:31–32; 1 Corinthians 11:32
10 Job 8:13–14; Micah 3:11; Deuteronomy 29:19; John 8:41
11 Matthew 7:22–23
12 1 John 2:3; 3:14, 18–19, 21, 24; 5:13
13 Romans 5:2, 5
14 Hebrews 6:11, 19
15 Hebrews 6:17–18
16 2 Peter 1:4–5, 10–11; 1 John 2:3; 3:14; 2 Corinthians 1:12

are the children of God:[1] which Spirit is the earnest [the pledge] of our inheritance, whereby we are sealed to the day of redemption.[2]

3. This infallible assurance does not so belong to the essence of faith, but that a true believer may wait long, and conflict with many difficulties, before he be partaker of it:[3] yet, being enabled by the Spirit to know the things which are freely given him of God, he may, without extraordinary revelation in the right use of ordinary means, attain thereunto.[4] And therefore it is the duty of every one to give all diligence to make his calling and election sure;[5] that thereby his heart may be enlarged in peace and joy in the Holy Spirit, in love and thankfulness to God, and in strength and cheerfulness in the duties of obedience,[6] the proper fruits of this assurance; so far is it from inclining men to looseness.[7]

4. True believers may have the assurance of their salvation divers [various] ways shaken, diminished, and intermitted [temporarily lost]; as, by negligence in preserving of it, by falling into some special sin which wounds the conscience and grieves the Spirit; by some sudden or vehement temptation, by God's withdrawing the light of His countenance, and suffering even such as fear Him to walk in darkness and to have no light:[8] yet are they never so utterly destitute of that seed of God, and life of faith, that love of Christ and the brethren, that sincerity of heart, and conscience of duty, out of which, by the operation of the Spirit, this assurance may, in due time, be revived;[9] and by the which, in the meantime, they are supported from utter despair.[10]

1   Romans 8:15–16
2   Ephesians 1:13–14; 4:30; 2 Corinthians 1:21–22
3   1 John 5:13; Isaiah 50:10; Mark 9:24, Psalm 88; 77:1–12
4   1 Corinthians 2:12; 1 John 4:13; Hebrews 6:11–12; Ephesians 3:17–19
5   2 Peter 1:10
6   Romans 5:1–2, 5; 14:17; 15:13; Ephesians 1:3–4; Psalm 4:6–7; 119:32
7   1 John 2:1–2; Romans 6:1–2; Titus 2:11–12, 14; 2 Corinthians 7:1; Romans 8:1, 12; 1 John 3:2–3; Psalm 130:4; 1 John 1:6–7
8   Song of Solomon 5:2–3, 6; Psalm 51:8, 12, 14; Ephesians 4:30–31; Psalm 77:1–10; Matthew 26:69–72; Psalm 31:22; Psalm 88; Isaiah 50:10
9   1 John 3:9; Luke 22:32; Job 13:15; Psalm 73:15; 51:8, 12; Isaiah 50:10
10   Micah 7:7–9; Jeremiah 32:40; Isaiah 54:7–10; Psalm 22:1; Psalm 88

Chapter 19

Of the Law of God

1. God gave to Adam a law, as a covenant of works, by which He bound him and all his posterity, to personal, entire, exact, and perpetual obedience; promised life upon the fulfilling, and threatened death upon the breach of it: and endued him with power and ability to keep it.[1]

2. This law, after his fall, continued to be a perfect rule of righteousness; and, as such, was delivered by God upon Mount Sinai, in ten commandments, and written in two tables:[2] the first four commandments containing our duty towards God; and the other six, our duty to man.[3]

3. Besides this law, commonly called moral, God was pleased to give to the people of Israel, as a church under age, ceremonial laws, containing several typical ordinances, partly of worship, prefiguring Christ, His graces, actions, sufferings, and benefits;[4] and partly, holding forth divers [various] instructions of moral duties.[5] All which ceremonial laws are now abrogated, under the New Testament.[6]

4. To them also, as a body politic, He gave sundry judicial laws, which expired together with the State of that people; not obliging any other now, further than the general equity thereof may require.[7]

5. The moral law does forever bind all, as well justified persons as others, to the obedience thereof;[8] and that, not only in regard of the matter contained in it, but also in respect of the authority of God the Creator, who gave it:[9] neither does Christ, in the Gospel, any way dissolve, but much strengthen this obligation.[10]

6. Although true believers be not under the law, as a covenant of

---

1   Genesis 1:26-27 with Genesis 2:17; Romans 2:14-15; 10:5; 5:12, 19; Galatians 3:10, 12; Ecclesiastes 7:29; Job 28:28
2   James 1:25; 2:8, 10-12; Romans 13:8-9; Deuteronomy 5:32; 10:4; Exodus 34:1
3   Matthew 22:37-40
4   Hebrews 9; 10:1; Galatians 4:1-3; Colossians 2:17
5   1 Corinthians 5:7; 2 Corinthians 6:17; Jude 23
6   Colossians 2:14, 16-17; Daniel 9:27; Ephesians 2:15-16
7   Exodus 21; 22:1-29; Genesis 49:10 with 1 Peter 2:13-14; Matthew 5:17, 38-39; 1 Corinthians 9:8-10
8   Romans 13:8-10; Ephesians 6:2; 1 John 2:3-4, 7-8
9   James 2:10-11
10 Matthew 5:17-19; James 2:8; Romans 3:31

works, to be thereby justified, or condemned;[1] yet is it of great use to them, as well as to others; in that, as a rule of life informing them of the will of God, and their duty, it directs and binds them to walk accordingly;[2] discovering also the sinful pollutions of their nature, hearts and lives;[3] so as, examining themselves thereby, they may come to further conviction of, humiliation for, and hatred against sin;[4] together with a clearer sight of the need they have of Christ, and the perfection of His obedience.[5] It is likewise of use to the regenerate, to restrain their corruptions, in that it forbids sin:[6] and the threatenings of it serve to show what even their sins deserve; and what afflictions, in this life, they may expect for them, although freed from the curse thereof threatened in the law.[7] The promises of it, in like manner, show them God's approbation of obedience, and what blessings they may expect upon the performance thereof:[8] although not as due to them by the law as a covenant of works.[9] So as, a man's doing good, and refraining from evil, because the law encourages to the one and deters from the other, is no evidence of his being under the law: and not under grace.[10]

7. Neither are the aforementioned uses of the law contrary to the grace of the Gospel, but do sweetly comply with it;[11] the Spirit of Christ subduing and enabling the will of man to do that freely, and cheerfully, which the will of God, revealed in the law, requires to be done.[12]

Chapter 20
Of Christian Liberty, and Liberty of Conscience

1. The liberty which Christ has purchased for believers under the Gospel consists in their freedom from the guilt of sin, the condemning wrath of God, the curse of the moral law;[13] and, in their being delivered

---

1   Romans 6:14; Galatians 2:16; 3:13; 4:4–5; Acts 13:39; Romans 8:1
2   Romans 7:12, 22, 25; Psalm 119:4–6; 1 Corinthians 7:19; Galatians 5:14, 16, 18–23
3   Romans 7:7; 3:20
4   James 1:23–25; Romans 7:9, 14, 24
5   Galatians 3:24; Romans 7:24–25; 8:3–4
6   James 2:11; Psalm 119:101, 104, 128
7   Ezra 9:13–14; Psalm 89:30–34
8   Leviticus 26:1–14; 2 Corinthians 6:16; Ephesians 6:2–3; Psalm 37:11; Matthew 5:5; Psalm 19:11
9   Galatians 2:16; Luke 17:10
10 Romans 6:12, 14; 1 Peter 3:8–12; Psalm 34:12–16; Hebrews 12:28–29
11 Galatians 3:21
12 Ezekiel 36:27; Hebrews 8:10; Jeremiah 31:33
13 Titus 2:14; 1 Thessalonians 1:10; Galatians 3:13

from this present evil world, bondage to Satan, and dominion of sin;[1] from the evil of afflictions, the sting of death, the victory of the grave, and everlasting damnation;[2] as also, in their free access to God,[3] and their yielding obedience unto Him, not out of slavish fear, but a child-like love and willing mind.[4] All which were common also to believers under the law.[5] But, under the New Testament, the liberty of Christians is further enlarged, in their freedom from the yoke of the ceremonial law, to which the Jewish Church was subjected;[6] and in greater boldness of access to the throne of grace,[7] and in fuller communications of the free Spirit of God, than believers under the law did ordinarily partake of.[8]

2. God alone is Lord of the conscience,[9] and has left it free from the doctrines and commandments of men, which are, in anything, contrary to His Word; or beside it, if matters of faith, or worship.[10] So that, to believe such doctrines, or to obey such commands, out of conscience, is to betray true liberty of conscience:[11] and the requiring of an implicit faith, and an absolute and blind obedience, is to destroy liberty of conscience, and reason also.[12]

3. They who, upon pretence of Christian liberty, do practice any sin, or cherish any lust, do thereby destroy the end of Christian liberty, which is, that being delivered out of the hands of our enemies, we might serve the Lord without fear, in holiness and righteousness before Him, all the days of our life.[13]

4. And because the powers which God has ordained, and the liberty which Christ has purchased are not intended by God to destroy, but mutually to uphold and preserve one another; they who, upon pretence

---

1 Galatians 1:4; Colossians 1:13; Acts 26:18; Romans 6:14
2 Romans 8:28; Psalm 119:71; 1 Corinthians 15:54–57; Romans 8:1
3 Romans 5:1–2
4 Romans 8:14–15; 1 John 4:18
5 Galatians 3:9, 14
6 Galatians 4:1–3, 6–7; 5:1; Acts 15:10–11
7 Hebrews 4:14, 16; Hebrews 10:19–22
8 John 7:38–39; 2 Corinthians 3:13, 17–18
9 James 4:12; Romans 14:4
10 Acts 4:19; 5:29; 1 Corinthians 7:23; Matthew 23:8–10; 2 Corinthians 1:24; Matthew 15:9
11 Colossians 2:20, 22–23; Galatians 1:10; 2:4–5; 5:1
12 Romans 10:17; 14:23; Isaiah 8:20; Acts 17:11; John 4:22; Hosea 5:11; Revelation 13:12, 16–17; Jeremiah 8:9
13 Galatians 5:13; 1 Peter 2:16; 2 Peter 2:19; John 8:34; Luke 1:74–75

of Christian liberty, shall oppose any lawful power, or the lawful exercise of it, whether it be civil or ecclesiastical, resist the ordinance of God.[1] And, for their publishing of such opinions, or maintaining of such practices, as are contrary to the light of nature, or to the known principles of Christianity (whether concerning faith, worship, or conversation), or to the power of godliness; or, such erroneous opinions or practices, as either in their own nature, or in the manner of publishing or maintaining them, are destructive to the external peace and order which Christ has established in the Church, they may lawfully be called to account,[2] and proceeded against, by the censures of the Church, and by the power of the civil magistrate.[3]

Chapter 21

Of Religious Worship, and the Sabbath Day

1. The light of nature shows that there is a God, who has lordship and sovereignty over all, is good, and does good unto all, and is therefore to be feared, loved, praised, called upon, trusted in, and served, with all the heart, and with all the soul, and with all the might.[4] But the acceptable way of worshipping the true God is instituted by Himself, and so limited by His own revealed will, that He may not be worshipped according to the imaginations and devices of men, or the suggestions of Satan, under any visible representation, or any other way not prescribed in the holy Scripture.[5]

2. Religious worship is to be given to God, the Father, Son, and Holy Spirit; and to Him alone;[6] not to angels, saints, or any other creature:[7] and, since the fall, not without a Mediator; nor in the mediation of any other but of Christ alone.[8]

---

1   Matthew 12:25; 1 Peter 2:13–14, 16; Romans 13:1–8; Hebrews 13:17
2   Romans 1:32; 1 Corinthians 5:1, 5, 11, 13; 2 John 10–11; 2 Thessalonians 3:14; 1 Timothy 6:3–5; Titus 1:10–11, 13; 3:10; Matthew 18:15–17; 1 Timothy 1:19–20; Revelation 2:2, 14–15, 20; 3:9
3   Deuteronomy 13:6–12; Romans 13:3–4; 2 John 10–11; Ezra 7:23, 25–28; Revelation 17:12, 16–17; Nehemiah 13:15, 17, 21–22, 25, 30; 2 Kings 23:5–6, 9, 20–21; 2 Chronicles 34:33; 15:12–13, 16; Daniel 3:29; 1 Timothy 2:2; Isaiah 49:23; Zechariah 13:2–3
4   Romans 1:20; Acts 17:24; Psalm 119:68; Jeremiah 10:7; Psalm 31:23; 18:3; Romans 10:12; Psalm 62:8; Joshua 24:14; Mark 12:33
5   Deuteronomy 12:32; Matthew 15:9; Acts 17:25; Matthew 4:9–10; Deuteronomy 4:15–20; Exodus 20:4–6; Colossians 2:23
6   Matthew 4:10 with John 5:23 and 2 Corinthians 13:14
7   Colossians 2:18; Revelation 19:10; Romans 1:25
8   John 14:6; 1 Timothy 2:5; Ephesians 2:18; Colossians 3:17

3. Prayer, with thanksgiving, being one special part of religious worship,[1] is by God required of all men:[2] and, that it may be accepted, it is to be made in the name of the Son,[3] by the help of His Spirit,[4] according to His will,[5] with understanding, reverence, humility, fervency, faith, love and perseverance;[6] and, if vocal, in a known tongue.[7]

4. Prayer is to be made for things lawful;[8] and for all sorts of men living, or that shall live hereafter:[9] but not for the dead,[10] nor for those of whom it may be known that they have sinned the sin unto death.[11]

5. The reading of the Scriptures with godly fear;[12] the sound preaching[13] and conscionable hearing of the Word, in obedience to God, with understanding, faith and reverence;[14] singing of psalms with grace in the heart;[15] as also, the due administration and worthy receiving of the sacraments instituted by Christ; are all parts of the ordinary religious worship of God:[16] beside religious oaths,[17] vows,[18] solemn fastings,[19] and thanksgivings upon special occasions,[20] which are, in their several times and seasons, to be used in a holy and religious manner.[21]

6. Neither prayer, nor any other part of religious worship, is now, under the Gospel, either tied unto, or made more acceptable by any place in which it is performed, or towards which it is directed:[22] but God is to

---

1   Philippians 4:6
2   Psalm 65:2
3   John 14:13–14; 1 Peter 2:5
4   Romans 8:26
5   1 John 5:14
6   Psalm 47:7; Ecclesiastes 5:1–2; Hebrews 12:28; Genesis 18:27; James 5:16; 1:6–7; Mark 11:24; Matthew 6:12, 14–15; Colossians 4:2; Ephesians 6:18
7   1 Corinthians 14:14
8   1 John 5:14
9   1 Timothy 2:1–2; John 17:20; 2 Samuel 7:29; Ruth 4:12
10   2 Samuel 12:21–23 with Luke 16:25–26; Revelation 14:13
11   1 John 5:16
12   Acts 15:21; Revelation 1:3
13   2 Timothy 4:2
14   James 1:22; Acts 10:33; Matthew 13:19; Hebrews 4:2; Isaiah 66:2
15   Colossians 3:16; Ephesians 5:19; James 5:13
16   Matthew 28:19; 1 Corinthians 11:23–29; Acts 2:42
17   Deuteronomy 6:13 with Nehemiah 10:29
18   Isaiah 19:21 with Ecclesiastes 5:4–5
19   Joel 2:12; Esther 4:16; Matthew 9:15; 1 Corinthians 7:5
20   Psalm 107; Esther 9:22
21   Hebrews 12:28
22   John 4:21

be worshipped everywhere,[1] in spirit and truth;[2] as, in private families[3] daily,[4] and in secret, each one by himself;[5] so, more solemnly in the public assemblies, which are not carelessly or wilfully to be neglected, or forsaken, when God, by His Word or providence, calls thereunto.[6]

7. As it is the law of nature, that, in general, a due proportion of time be set apart for the worship of God; so, in His Word, by a positive, moral, and perpetual commandment, binding all men in all ages, He has particularly appointed one day in seven, for a Sabbath, to be kept holy unto Him:[7] which, from the beginning of the world to the resurrection of Christ, was the last day of the week: and, from the resurrection of Christ, was changed into the first day of the week,[8] which, in Scripture, is called the Lord's Day,[9] and is to be continued to the end of the world, as the Christian Sabbath.[10]

8. This Sabbath is to be kept holy unto the Lord when men, after a due preparing of their hearts, and ordering of their common affairs beforehand, do not only observe a holy rest all the day from their own works, words, and thoughts about their worldly employments and recreations,[11] but also are taken up the whole time in the public and private exercises of His worship, and in the duties of necessity and mercy.[12]

Chapter 22

Of Lawful Oaths and Vows

1. A lawful oath is a part of religious worship,[13] wherein, upon just occasion, the person swearing solemnly calls God to witness what

---

1   Malachi 1:11; 1 Timothy 2:8
2   John 4:23–24
3   Jeremiah 10:25; Deuteronomy 6:6–7; Job 1:5; 2 Samuel 6:18, 20; 1 Peter 3:7; Acts 10:2
4   Matthew 6:11
5   Matthew 6:6; Ephesians 6:18
6   Isaiah 56:6–7; Hebrews 10:25; Proverbs 1:20-21,-24; 8:34; Acts 13:42; Luke 4:16; Acts 2:42
7   Exodus 20:8, 10–11; Isaiah 56:2, 4, 6–7
8   Genesis 2:2–3; 1 Corinthians 16:1–2; Acts 20:7
9   Revelation 1:10
10 Exodus 20:8, 10 with Matthew 5:17–18
11 Exodus 20:8; 16:23, 25–26, 29–30; 31:15–17; Isaiah 58:13; Nehemiah 13:15–19, 21–22
12 Isaiah 58:13; Matthew 12:1–13
13 Deuteronomy 10:20

he asserts, or promises, and to judge him according to the truth or falsehood of what he swears.[1]

2. The name of God only is that by which men ought to swear, and therein it is to be used with all holy fear and reverence.[2] Therefore, to swear vainly, or rashly, by that glorious and dreadful Name; or, to swear at all by any other thing, is sinful, and to be abhorred.[3] Yet, as in matters of weight and moment, an oath is warranted by the Word of God, under the New Testament as well as under the Old;[4] so a lawful oath, being imposed by lawful authority, in such matters ought to be taken.[5]

3. Whosoever takes an oath ought duly to consider the weightiness of so solemn an act, and therein to avouch [affirm] nothing but what he is fully persuaded is the truth:[6] neither may any man bind himself by oath to anything but what is good and just, and what he believes so to be, and what he is able and resolved to perform.[7] Yet it is a sin to refuse an oath touching anything that is good and just, being imposed by lawful authority.[8]

4. An oath is to be taken in the plain and common sense of the words, without equivocation, or mental reservation.[9] It cannot oblige to sin; but in anything not sinful, being taken, it binds to performance, although to a man's own hurt.[10] Nor is it to be violated, although made to heretics, or infidels.[11]

5. A vow is of the like nature with a promissory oath [promise], and ought to be made with the like religious care, and to be performed with the like faithfulness.[12]

6. It is not to be made to any creature, but to God alone:[13] and that it may be accepted, it is to be made voluntarily, out of faith, and conscience

1 Exodus 20:7; Leviticus 19:12; 2 Corinthians 1:23; 2 Chronicles 6:22–23
2 Deuteronomy 6:13
3 Exodus 20:7; Jeremiah 5:7; Matthew 5:34, 37; James 5:12
4 Hebrews 6:16; 2 Corinthians 1:23; Isaiah 65:16
5 1 Kings 8:31; Nehemiah 13:25; Ezra 10:5
6 Exodus 20:7; Jeremiah 4:2
7 Genesis 24:2–3, 5–6, 8–9
8 Numbers 5:19, 21; Nehemiah 5:12; Exodus 22:7–11
9 Jeremiah 4:2; Psalm 24:4
10 1 Samuel 25:22, 32–34; Psalm 15:4
11 Ezekiel 17:16, 18–19; Joshua 9:18–19 with 2 Samuel 21:1
12 Isaiah 19:21; Ecclesiastes 5:4–6; Psalm 61:8; 66:13–14
13 Psalm 76:11; Jeremiah 44:25–26

of duty, in way of thankfulness for mercy received, or for the obtaining of what we want; whereby we more strictly bind ourselves to necessary duties; or, to other things, so far and so long as they may fitly conduce [contribute] thereunto.[1]

7. No man may vow to do anything forbidden in the Word of God, or what would hinder any duty therein commanded, or which is not in his own power, and for the performance whereof he has no promise of ability from God.[2] In which respects, Popish monastical vows of perpetual single life, professed poverty, and regular obedience, are so far from being degrees of higher perfection, that they are superstitious and sinful snares, in which no Christian may entangle himself.[3]

Chapter 23

Of the Civil Magistrate

1. God, the supreme Lord and King of all the world, has ordained civil magistrates, to be, under Him, over the people, for His own glory, and the public good: and, to this end, has armed them with the power of the sword, for the defence and encouragement of them that are good, and for the punishment of evil doers.[4]

2. It is lawful for Christians to accept and execute the office of a magistrate, when called thereunto;[5] in the managing whereof, as they ought especially to maintain piety, justice, and peace, according to the wholesome laws of each commonwealth;[6] so, for that end, they may lawfully now, under the New Testament, wage war, upon just and necessary occasion.[7]

3. Civil magistrates may not assume to themselves the administration of the Word and sacraments, or the power of the keys of the kingdom of heaven;[8] yet he has authority, and it is his duty, to take order that unity and peace be preserved in the Church, that the truth of God be

---

1   Deuteronomy 23:21-23; Psalm 50:14; Genesis 28:20-22; 1 Samuel 1:11; Psalm 66:13-14; 132:2-5
2   Acts 23:12, 14; Mark 6:26; Numbers 30:5, 8, 12-13
3   Matthew 19:11-12; 1 Corinthians 7:2, 9; Ephesians 4:28; 1 Peter 4:2; 1 Corinthians 7:23
4   Romans 13:1-4; 1 Peter 2:13-14
5   Proverbs 8:15-16; Romans 13:1-2, 4
6   Psalm 2:10-12; 1 Timothy 2:2; Psalm 82:3-4; 2 Samuel 23:3; 1 Peter 2:13
7   Luke 3:14; Romans 13:4; Matthew 8:9-10; Acts 10:1-2; Revelation 17:14, 16
8   2 Chronicles 26:18 with Matthew 18:17 and Matthew 16:19; 1 Corinthians 12:28-29; Ephesians 4:11-12; 1 Corinthians 4:1-2; Romans 10:15; Hebrews 5:4

kept pure and entire, that all blasphemies and heresies be suppressed, all corruptions and abuses in worship and discipline prevented or reformed, and all the ordinances of God duly settled, administered, and observed.[1] For the better effecting whereof, he has power to call synods, to be present at them and to provide that whatsoever is transacted in them be according to the mind of God.[2]

4. It is the duty of people to pray for magistrates,[3] to honour their persons,[4] to pay them tribute and other dues,[5] to obey their lawful commands, and to be subject to their authority, for conscience' sake.[6] Infidelity, or difference in religion, does not make void the magistrates' just and legal authority, nor free the people from their due obedience to them:[7] from which ecclesiastical persons are not exempted,[8] much less has the Pope any power and jurisdiction over them in their dominions, or over any of their people; and, least of all, to deprive them of their dominions, or lives, if he shall judge them to be heretics, or upon any other pretence whatsoever.[9]

Chapter 24

Of Marriage and Divorce

1. Marriage is to be between one man and one woman: neither is it lawful for any man to have more than one wife, nor for any woman to have more than one husband, at the same time.[10]

2. Marriage was ordained for the mutual help of husband and wife,[11] for the increase of mankind with a legitimate issue, and of the Church with a holy seed;[12] and for preventing of uncleanness.[13]

---

1   Isaiah 49:23; Psalm 122:9; Ezra 7:23, 25–28; Leviticus 24:16; Deuteronomy 13:5–6, 12; 2 Kings 18:4; 1 Chronicles 13:1–9; 2 Kings 23:1–26; 2 Chronicles 34:33; 15:12–13
2   2 Chronicles 19:8–11; 2 Chronicles 29 and 30; Matthew 2:4–5
3   1 Timothy 2:1–2
4   1 Peter 2:17
5   Romans 13:6–7
6   Romans 13:5; Titus 3:1
7   1 Peter 2:13–14, 16
8   Romans 13:1; 1 Kings 2:35; Acts 25:9–11; 2 Peter 2:1, 10–11; Jude 8–11
9   2 Thessalonians 2:4; Revelation 13:15–17
10 Genesis 2:24; Matthew 19:5–6; Proverbs 2:17
11 Genesis 2:18
12 Malachi 2:15
13 1 Corinthians 7:2, 9

3. It is lawful for all sorts of people to marry, who are able with judgment to give their consent.[1] Yet it is the duty of Christians to marry only in the Lord:[2] and therefore such as profess the true reformed religion should not marry with infidels, papists, or other idolaters: neither should such as are godly be unequally yoked, by marrying with such as are notoriously wicked in their life, or maintain damnable heresies.[3]

4. Marriage ought not to be within the degrees of consanguinity or affinity forbidden by the Word;[4] nor can such incestuous marriages ever be made lawful by any law of man or consent of parties, so as those persons may live together as man and wife.[5] The man may not marry any of his wife's kindred, nearer in blood then he may of his own; nor the woman of her husband's kindred, nearer in blood than of her own.[6]

5. Adultery or fornication committed after a contract, being detected before marriage, gives just occasion to the innocent party to dissolve that contract.[7] In the case of adultery after marriage, it is lawful for the innocent party to sue out a divorce and, after the divorce,[8] to marry another, as if the offending party were dead.[9]

6. Although the corruption of man be such as is apt to study arguments unduly to put asunder those whom God has joined together in marriage: yet, nothing but adultery, or such wilful desertion as can no way be remedied by the Church, or civil magistrate, is cause sufficient of dissolving the bond of marriage:[10] wherein, a public and orderly course of proceeding is to be observed; and the persons concerned in it not left to their own wills, and discretion, in their own case.[11]

---

1 Hebrews 13:4; 1 Timothy 4:3; 1 Corinthians 7:36-38; Genesis 24:57-58
2 1 Corinthians 7:39
3 Genesis 34:14; Exodus 34:16; Deuteronomy 7:3-4; 1 Kings 11:4; Nehemiah 13:25-27; Malachi 2:11-12; 2 Corinthians 6:14
4 Leviticus 18; 1 Corinthians 5:1; Amos 2:7
5 Mark 6:18; Leviticus 18:24-28
6 Leviticus 20:19-21
7 Matthew 1:18-20
8 Matthew 5:31-32
9 Matthew 19:9; Romans 7:2-3
10 Matthew 19:8-9; 1 Corinthians 7:15; Matthew 19:6
11 Deuteronomy 24:1-4

Chapter 25

Of the Church

1. The catholic or universal Church, which is invisible, consists of the whole number of the elect, that have been, are, or shall be gathered into one, under Christ the Head thereof; and is the spouse, the body, the fullness of Him that fills all in all.[1]

2. The visible Church, which is also catholic or universal under the Gospel (not confined to one nation, as before under the law), consists of all those throughout the world that profess the true religion;[2] and of their children:[3] and is the kingdom of the Lord Jesus Christ,[4] the house and family of God,[5] out of which there is no ordinary possibility of salvation.[6]

3. Unto this catholic visible Church Christ has given the ministry, oracles, and ordinances of God, for the gathering and perfecting of the saints, in this life, to the end of the world: and does, by His own presence and Spirit, according to His promise, make them effectual thereunto.[7]

4. This catholic Church has been sometimes more, sometimes less visible.[8] And particular Churches, which are members thereof, are more or less pure, according as the doctrine of the Gospel is taught and embraced, ordinances administered, and public worship performed more or less purely in them.[9]

5. The purest Churches under heaven are subject both to mixture and error;[10] and some have so degenerated, as to become no Churches of Christ, but synagogues of Satan.[11] Nevertheless, there shall be always a Church on earth to worship God according to His will.[12]

---

1   Ephesians 1:10, 22–23; 5:23, 27, 32; Colossians 1:18
2   1 Corinthians 1:2; 12:12–13; Psalm 2:8; Revelation 7:9; Romans 15:9–12
3   1 Corinthians 7:14; Acts 2:39; Ezekiel 16:20–21; Romans 11:16; Genesis 3:15; 17:7
4   Matthew 13:47; Isaiah 9:7
5   Ephesians 2:19; 3:15
6   Acts 2:47
7   1 Corinthians 12:28; Ephesians 4:11–13; Matthew 28:19–20; Isaiah 59:21
8   Romans 11:3–4; Revelation 12:6, 14
9   Revelation 2 and 3; 1 Corinthians 5:6–7
10 1 Corinthians 13:12; Revelation 2 and 3; Matthew 13:24–30, 47
11 Revelation 18:2; Romans 11:18–22
12 Matthew 16:18, Psalm 72:17; 102:28; Matthew 28:19–20

6. There is no other head of the Church but the Lord Jesus Christ;[1] nor can the Pope of Rome, in any sense, be head thereof; but is that Antichrist, that man of sin, and son of perdition, that exalts himself, in the Church, against Christ and all that is called God.[2]

Chapter 26

Of the Communion of Saints

1. All saints, that are united to Jesus Christ their Head, by His Spirit, and by faith, have fellowship with Him in His graces, sufferings, death, resurrection, and glory:[3] and, being united to one another in love, they have communion in each other's gifts and graces,[4] and are obliged to the performance of such duties, public and private, as do conduce to their mutual good, both in the inward and outward man.[5]

2. Saints by profession are bound to maintain a holy fellowship and communion in the worship of God, and in performing such other spiritual services as tend to their mutual edification;[6] as also in relieving each other in outward things, according to their several abilities and necessities. Which communion, as God offers opportunity, is to be extended unto all those who, in every place, call upon the name of the Lord Jesus.[7]

3. This communion which the saints have with Christ, does not make them in any wise partakers of the substance of His Godhead; or to be equal with Christ in any respect: either of which to affirm is impious and blasphemous.[8] Nor does their communion one with another, as saints, take away, or infringe the title or propriety which each man has in his goods and possessions.[9]

---

1   Colossians 1:18; Ephesians 1:22
2   Matthew 23:8-10; 2 Thessalonians 2:3-4, 8-9; Revelation 13:6
3   1 John 1:3; Ephesians 3:16-19; John 1:16; Ephesians 2:5-6; Philippians 3:10; Romans 6:5-6; 2 Timothy 2:12
4   Ephesians 4:15-16; 1 Corinthians 12:7; 3:21-23; Colossians 2:19
5   1 Thessalonians 5:11, 14; Romans 1:11-12, 14; 1 John 3:16-18; Galatians 6:10
6   Hebrews 10:24-25; Acts 2:42, 46; Isaiah 2:3; 1 Corinthians 11:20
7   Acts 2:44-45; 1 John 3:17; 2 Corinthians 8 and 9; Acts 11:29-30
8   Colossians 1:18; 1 Corinthians 8:6; Isaiah 42:8; 1 Timothy 6:15-16; Psalm 45:7 with Hebrews 1:8-9
9   Exodus 20:15; Ephesians 4:28; Acts 5:4

Chapter 27

Of the Sacraments

1. Sacraments are holy signs and seals of the covenant of grace,[1] immediately instituted by God,[2] to represent Christ and His benefits; and to confirm our interest in Him;[3] as also, to put a visible difference between those that belong unto the Church and the rest of the world;[4] and solemnly to engage them to the service of God in Christ, according to His Word.[5]

2. There is, in every sacrament, a spiritual relation, or sacramental union, between the sign and the thing signified: whence it comes to pass, that the names and effects of the one are attributed to the other.[6]

3. The grace which is exhibited in or by the sacraments rightly used, is not conferred by any power in them; neither does the efficacy of a sacrament depend upon the piety or intention of him that does administer it:[7] but upon the work of the Spirit,[8] and the word of institution, which contains, together with a precept authorizing the use thereof, a promise of benefit to worthy receivers.[9]

4. There are only two sacraments ordained by Christ our Lord in the Gospel; that is to say, Baptism, and the Supper of the Lord: neither of which may be dispensed by any, but by a minister of the Word lawfully ordained.[10]

5. The sacraments of the Old Testament in regard to the spiritual things thereby signified and exhibited, were, for substance, the same with those of the new.[11]

---

1 Romans 4:11; Genesis 17:7, 10
2 Matthew 28:19; 1 Corinthians 11:23
3 1 Corinthians 10:16; 11:25-26; Galatians 3:17
4 Romans 15:8; Exodus 12:48; Genesis 34:14
5 Romans 6:3-4; 1 Corinthians 10:16, 21
6 Genesis 17:10; Matthew 26:27-28; Titus 3:5
7 Romans2:28-29; 1 Peter 3:21
8 Matthew 3:11; 1 Corinthians 12:13
9 Matthew 26:27-28; 28:19-20
10 Matthew 28:19; 1 Corinthians 11:20, 23; 4:1; Hebrews 5:4
11 1 Corinthians 10:1-4

Chapter 28

Of Baptism

1. Baptism is a sacrament of the New Testament, ordained by Jesus Christ,[1] not only for the solemn admission of the party baptized into the visible Church;[2] but also to be unto him a sign and seal of the covenant of grace,[3] of his ingrafting into Christ,[4] of regeneration,[5] of remission of sins,[6] and of his giving up unto God, through Jesus Christ, to walk in newness of life.[7] Which sacrament is, by Christ's own appointment, to be continued in His Church until the end of the world.[8]

2. The outward element to be used in this sacrament is water, wherewith the party is to be baptized, in the name of the Father, and of the Son, and of the Holy Spirit, by a minister of the Gospel, lawfully called thereunto.[9]

3. Dipping of the person into the water is not necessary; but Baptism is rightly administered by pouring, or sprinkling water upon the person.[10]

4. Not only those that do actually profess faith in and obedience unto Christ,[11] but also the infants of one, or both, believing parents, are to be baptized.[12]

5. Although it is a great sin to contemn [disdain] or neglect this ordinance,[13] yet grace and salvation are not so inseparably annexed unto it, as that no person can be regenerated, or saved, without it:[14] or, that all that are baptized are undoubtedly regenerated.[15]

---

1 Matthew 28:19
2 1 Corinthians 12:13
3 Romans 4:11 with Colossians 2:11–12
4 Galatians 3:27; Romans 6:5
5 Titus 3:5
6 Mark 1:14
7 Romans 6:3–4
8 Matthew 28:19–20
9 Matthew 3:11; John 1:33; Matthew 28:19–20
10 Hebrews 9:10, 19–22; Acts 2:41; Acts 16:33; Mark 7:4
11 Mark 16:15–16; Acts 8:37–38
12 Genesis 17:7, 9–10 with Galatians 3:9, 14 and Colossians 2:11–12 and Acts 2:38–39 and Romans 4:11–12; 1 Corinthians 7:14; Matthew 28:19; Mark 10:13–16; Luke 18:15
13 Luke 7:30 with Exodus 4:24–26
14 Romans 4:11; Acts 10:2, 4, 22, 31, 45, 47
15 Acts 8:13, 23

6. The efficacy of Baptism is not tied to that moment of time wherein it is administered;[1] yet, notwithstanding, by the right use of this ordinance, the grace promised is not only offered, but really exhibited, and conferred, by the Holy Spirit, to such (whether of age or infants) as that grace belongs unto, according to the counsel of God's own will, in His appointed time.[2]

7. The sacrament of Baptism is but once to be administered unto any person.[3]

Chapter 29

Of the Lord's Supper

1. Our Lord Jesus, in the night wherein He was betrayed, instituted the sacrament of His body and blood, called the Lord's Supper, to be observed in His Church, unto the end of the world, for the perpetual remembrance of the sacrifice of Himself in His death; the sealing all benefits thereof unto true believers, their spiritual nourishment and growth in Him, their further engagement in and to all duties which they owe unto Him; and, to be a bond and pledge of their communion with Him, and with each other, as members of His mystical body.[4]

2. In this sacrament, Christ is not offered up to His Father; nor any real sacrifice made at all, for remission of sins of the quick [living] or dead;[5] but only a commemoration of that one offering up of Himself, by Himself, upon the cross, once for all: and a spiritual oblation [offering] of all possible praise unto God, for the same:[6] so that the Popish sacrifice of the mass (as they call it) is most abominably injurious to Christ's one, only sacrifice, the alone propitiation for all the sins of His elect.[7]

3. The Lord Jesus has, in this ordinance, appointed His ministers to declare His word of institution to the people; to pray, and bless the elements of bread and wine, and thereby to set them apart from a common to an holy use; and to take and break the bread, to take

---

1   John 3:5, 8
2   Galatians 3:27; Titus 3:5; Ephesians 5:25–26; Acts 2:38, 41
3   Titus 3:5
4   1 Corinthians 11:23–26; 10:16–17, 21; 12:13
5   Hebrews 9:22, 25–26, 28
6   1 Corinthians 11:24–26; Matthew 26:26–27
7   Hebrews 7:23–24, 27; 10:11–12, 14, 18

the cup, and (they communicating also themselves) to give both to the communicants;[1] but to none who are not then present in the congregation.[2]

4. Private masses, or receiving this sacrament by a priest, or any other alone;[3] as likewise, the denial of the cup to the people,[4] worshipping the elements, the lifting them up, or carrying them about, for adoration, and the reserving them for any pretended religious use; are all contrary to the nature of this sacrament, and to the institution of Christ.[5]

5. The outward elements in this sacrament, duly set apart to the uses ordained by Christ, have such relation to Him crucified, as that, truly, yet sacramentally only, they are sometimes called by the name of the things they represent, to wit, the body and blood of Christ;[6] albeit, in substance and nature, they still remain truly and only bread and wine, as they were before.[7]

6. That doctrine which maintains a change of the substance of bread and wine, into the substance of Christ's body and blood (commonly called transubstantiation) by consecration of a priest, or by any other way, is repugnant, not to Scripture alone, but even to common sense, and reason; overthrows the nature of the sacrament, and has been, and is, the cause of manifold superstitions; yes, of gross idolatries.[8]

7. Worthy receivers, outwardly partaking of the visible elements, in this sacrament,[9] do then also, inwardly by faith, really and indeed, yet not carnally and corporally but spiritually, receive and feed upon, Christ crucified, and all benefits of His death: the body and blood of Christ being then, not corporally or carnally, in, with, or under the bread and wine; yet, as really, but spiritually, present to the faith of believers in that ordinance, as the elements themselves are to their outward senses.[10]

8. Although ignorant and wicked men receive the outward elements

1 Matthew 26:26–28 and Mark 14:22–24 and Luke 22:19–20 with 1 Corinthians 11:23–26
2 Acts 20:7; 1 Corinthians 11:20
3 1 Corinthians 10:16
4 Mark 14:23; 1 Corinthians 11:25–29
5 Matthew 15:9
6 Matthew 26:26–28
7 1 Corinthians 11:26–28; Matthew 26:29
8 Acts 3:21 with 1 Corinthians 11:24–26; Luke 24:6, 39
9 1 Corinthians 11:28
10 1 Corinthians 10:16

in this sacrament; yet, they receive not the thing signified thereby; but, by their unworthy coming thereunto, are guilty of the body and blood of the Lord, to their own damnation. Wherefore, all ignorant and ungodly persons, as they are unfit to enjoy communion with Him, so are they unworthy of the Lord's table; and cannot, without great sin against Christ, while they remain such, partake of these holy mysteries,[1] or be admitted thereunto.[2]

Chapter 30

Of Church Censures

1. The Lord Jesus, as king and head of His Church, has therein appointed a government, in the hand of Church officers, distinct from the civil magistrate.[3]

2. To these officers the keys of the kingdom of heaven are committed; by virtue whereof, they have power, respectively, to retain, and remit sins; to shut that kingdom against the impenitent, both by the Word, and censures; and to open it unto penitent sinners, by the ministry of the Gospel; and by absolution from censures, as occasion shall require.[4]

3. Church censures are necessary, for the reclaiming and gaining of offending brethren, for deterring of others from the like offenses, for purging out of that leaven which might infect the whole lump, for vindicating the honour of Christ, and the holy profession of the Gospel, and for preventing the wrath of God, which might justly fall upon the Church, if they should suffer His covenant, and the seals thereof, to be profaned by notorious and obstinate offenders.[5]

4. For the better attaining of these ends, the officers of the Church are to proceed by admonition; suspension from the sacrament of the Lord's Supper for a season; and by excommunication from the Church; according to the nature of the crime, and demerit of the person.[6]

---

1   1 Corinthians 11:27-29; 2 Corinthians 6:14-16
2   1 Corinthians 5:6-7, 13; 2 Thessalonians 3:6, 14-15; Matthew 7:6
3   Isaiah 9:6-7; 1 Timothy 5:17; 1 Thessalonians 5:12; Acts 20:17, 28; Hebrews 13:7, 17, 24; 1 Corinthians 12:28; Matthew 28:18-20
4   Matthew 16:19; 18:17-18; John 20:21-23; 2 Corinthians 2:6-8
5   1 Corinthians 5; 1 Timothy 5:20; Matthew 7:6; 1 Timothy 1:20; 1 Corinthians 11:27-34 with Jude 23
6   1 Thessalonians 5:12; 2 Thessalonians 3:6, 14-15; 1 Corinthians 5:4-5, 13; Matthew 18:17; Titus 3:10

Chapter 31
Of Synods and Councils

1. For the better government, and further edification of the Church, there ought to be such assemblies as are commonly called synods or councils.[1]

2. As magistrates may lawfully call a synod of ministers, and other fit persons, to consult and advise with, about matters of religion;[2] so, if magistrates be open enemies to the Church, the ministers of Christ, of themselves, by virtue of their office, or they, with other fit persons upon delegation from their Churches, may meet together in such assemblies.[3]

3. It belongs to synods and councils, ministerially to determine controversies of faith, and cases of conscience; to set down rules and directions for the better ordering of the public worship of God, and government of His Church; to receive complaints in cases of maladministration, and authoritatively to determine the same: which decrees and determinations, if consonant to the Word of God, are to be received with reverence and submission; not only for their agreement with the Word, but also for the power whereby they are made, as being an ordinance of God appointed thereunto in His Word.[4]

4. All synods or councils, since the Apostles' times, whether general or particular, may err; and many have erred. Therefore they are not to be made the rule of faith, or practice; but to be used as a help in both.[5]

5. Synods and councils are to handle, or conclude, nothing, but that which is ecclesiastical: and are not to intermeddle [interfere] with civil affairs which concern the commonwealth; unless by way of humble petition in cases extraordinary; or, by way of advice, for satisfaction of conscience, if they be thereunto required by the civil magistrate.[6]

---

1 Acts 15:2, 4, 6
2 Isaiah 49:23; 1 Timothy 2:1–2; 2 Chronicles 19:8–11; 2 Chronicles 29 and 30; Matthew 2:4–5; Proverbs 11:14
3 Acts 15:2, 4, 22–23, 25
4 Acts 15:15, 19, 24, 27–31; 16:4; Matthew 18:17–20
5 Ephesians 2:20; Acts 17:11; 1 Corinthians 2:5; 2 Corinthians 1:24
6 Luke 12:13–14; John 18:36

The Westminster Confession of Faith in Modern English   51

Chapter 32

Of the State of Men after Death, and of the Resurrection of the Dead

1. The bodies of men, after death, return to dust, and see corruption:[1] but their souls, which neither die nor sleep, having an immortal subsistence, immediately return to God who gave them:[2] the souls of the righteous, being then made perfect in holiness, are received into the highest heavens, where they behold the face of God, in light and glory, waiting for the full redemption of their bodies.[3] And the souls of the wicked are cast into hell, where they remain in torments and utter darkness, reserved to the judgment of the great day.[4] Beside these two places, for souls separated from their bodies, the Scripture acknowledges none.

2. At the last day, such as are found alive shall not die, but be changed:[5] and all the dead shall be raised up, with the self-same bodies, and none other (although with different qualities), which shall be united again to their souls forever.[6]

3. The bodies of the unjust shall, by the power of Christ, be raised to dishonour: the bodies of the just, by His Spirit, unto honour; and be made conformable to His own glorious body.[7]

Chapter 33

Of the Last Judgment

1. God has appointed a day, wherein He will judge the world, in righteousness, by Jesus Christ,[8] to whom all power and judgment is given of the Father.[9] In which day, not only the apostate angels shall be judged,[10] but likewise all persons that have lived upon earth shall appear before the tribunal of Christ, to give an account of their thoughts,

---

1   Genesis 3:19; Acts 13:36
2   Luke 23:43; Ecclesiastes 12:7
3   Hebrews 12:23; 2 Corinthians 5:1, 6, 8; Philippians 1:23 with Acts 3:21 and Ephesians 4:10
4   Luke 16:23-24; Acts 1:25; Jude 6-7; 1 Peter 3:19
5   1 Thessalonians 4:17; 1 Corinthians 15:51-52
6   Job 19:26-27; 1 Corinthians 15:42-44
7   Acts 24:15; John 5:28-29; 1 Corinthians 15:43; Philippians 3:21
8   Acts 17:31
9   John 5:22, 27
10 1 Corinthians 6:3; Jude 6; 2 Peter 2:4

words, and deeds; and to receive according to what they have done in the body, whether good or evil.[1]

2. The end of God's appointing this day is for the manifestation of the glory of His mercy, in the eternal salvation of the elect; and of His justice, in the damnation of the reprobate, who are wicked and disobedient. For then shall the righteous go into everlasting life, and receive that fullness of joy and refreshing, which shall come from the presence of the Lord: but the wicked, who know not God, and obey not the Gospel of Jesus Christ, shall be cast into eternal torments, and be punished with everlasting destruction from the presence of the Lord, and from the glory of His power.[2]

3. As Christ would have us to be certainly persuaded that there shall be a day of judgment, both to deter all men from sin; and for the greater consolation of the godly in their adversity:[3] so will He have that day unknown to men, that they may shake off all carnal security, and be always watchful, because they know not at what hour the Lord will come; and may be ever prepared to say, Come Lord Jesus, come quickly, Amen.[4]

---

1   2 Corinthians 5:10; Ecclesiastes 12:14; Romans 2:16; 14:10, 12; Matthew 12:36–37
2   Matthew 25:31–46; Romans 2:5–6; 9:22–23; Matthew 25:21; Acts 3:19; 2 Thessalonians 1:7–10
3   2 Peter 3:11, 14; 2 Corinthians 5:10–11; 2 Thessalonians 1:5–7; Luke 21:27–28; Romans 8:23–25
4   Matthew 24:36, 42–44; Mark 13:35–37; Luke 12:35–36; Revelation 22:20

The Westminster Larger Catechism in Modern English

Q. 1. *What is the chief and highest end of man?*
A. Man's chief and highest end is to glorify God,[1] and fully to enjoy him forever.[2]

Q. 2. *How does it appear that there is a God?*
A. The very light of nature in man, and the works of God, declare plainly that there is a God;[3] but his word and Spirit only do sufficiently and effectually reveal him unto men for their salvation.[4]

Q. 3. *What is the Word of God?*
A. The holy Scriptures of the Old and New Testament are the Word of God,[5] the only rule of faith and obedience.[6]

Q. 4. *How does it appear that the Scriptures are the Word of God?*
A. The Scriptures manifest themselves to be the Word of God, by their majesty[7] and purity;[8] by the consent of all the parts,[9] and the scope of the whole, which is to give all glory to God;[10] by their light and power to convince and convert sinners, to comfort and build up believers unto salvation:[11] but the Spirit of God bearing witness by

---

1 Romans 11:36; 1 Corinthians 10:31
2 Psalm 73:24–28; John 17:21–23
3 Romans 1:19–20; Psalm 19:1–3; Acts 17:28
4 1 Corinthians 2:9–10; 2 Timothy 3:15–17; Isaiah 59:21
5 2 Timothy 3:16; 2 Peter 1:19–21
6 Ephesians 2:20; Revelation 22:18–19; Isaiah 8:20; Luke 16:29, 31; Galatians 1:8–9; 2 Timothy 3:15–16
7 Hosea 8:12; 1 Corinthians 2:6–7, 13; Psalm 119:18, 129
8 Psalm 12:6; Psalm 119:140
9 Acts 10:43; Acts 26:22
10 Romans 3:19, 27
11 Acts 18:28; Hebrews 4:12; James 1:18; Psalm 19:7–9; Romans 15:4; Acts 20:32

and with the Scriptures in the heart of man, is alone able fully to persuade it that they are the very word of God.[1]

Q. 5. *What do the Scriptures principally teach?*

A. The Scriptures principally teach, what man is to believe concerning God, and what duty God requires of man.[2]

What Man Ought to Believe Concerning God

Q. 6. *What do the Scriptures make known of God?*

A. The Scriptures make known what God is,[3] the persons in the Godhead,[4] his decrees,[5] and the execution of his decrees.[6]

Q. 7. *What is God?*

A. God is a Spirit,[7] in and of himself infinite in being,[8] glory,[9] blessedness,[10] and perfection;[11] all-sufficient,[12] eternal,[13] unchangeable,[14] incomprehensible,[15] everywhere present,[16] almighty,[17] knowing all things,[18] most wise,[19]most holy,[20] most just,[21] most merciful and gracious, long-suffering, and abundant in goodness and truth.[22]

---

1   John 16:13-14; 1 John 2:20, 27; John 20:31
2   2 Timothy 1:13
3   Hebrews 11:6
4   1 John 5:17
5   Acts 15:14-15, 18
6   Acts 4:27-28
7   John 4:24
8   Exodus 3:14; Job 11:7-9
9   Acts 7:2
10 1 Timothy 6:15
11 Matthew 5:48
12 Genesis 17:1
13 Psalm 90:2
14 Malachi 3:6; James 1:17
15 1 Kings 8:27
16 Psalm 139:1-13
17 Revelation 4:8
18 Hebrews 4:13; Psalm 147:5
19 Romans 16:27
20 Isaiah 6:3; Revelation 15:4
21 Deuteronomy 32:4
22 Exodus 34:6

Q. 8. *Are there more Gods than one?*
A. There is but one only, the living and true God.[1]

Q. 9. *How many persons are there in the Godhead?*
A. There are three persons in the Godhead, the Father, the Son, and the Holy Spirit; and these three are one true, eternal God, the same in substance, equal in power and glory; although distinguished by their personal properties.[2]

Q. 10. *What are the personal properties of the three persons in the Godhead?*
A. It is proper to the Father to beget the Son,[3] and to the Son to be begotten of the Father,[4] and to the Holy Spirit to proceed from the Father and the Son from all eternity.[5]

Q. 11. *How does it appear that the Son and the Holy Spirit are God equal with the Father?*
A. The Scriptures manifest that the Son and the Holy Spirit are God equal with the Father, ascribing unto them such names,[6] attributes,[7] works,[8] and worship,[9] as are proper to God only.

Q. 12. *What are the decrees of God?*
A. God's decrees are the wise, free, and holy acts of the counsel of his will,[10] whereby, from all eternity, he has, for his own glory, unchangeably foreordained whatsoever comes to pass in time,[11] especially concerning angels and men.

Q. 13. *What has God especially decreed concerning angels and men?*
A. God, by an eternal and immutable decree, out of his mere love, for the praise of his glorious grace, to be manifested in due time, has elected some angels to glory;[12] and in Christ has chosen some men

---

1   Deuteronomy 6:4; 1 Corinthians 8:4, 6; Jeremiah 10:10
2   1 John 5:7; Matthew 3:16–17; 28:19; 2 Corinthians 13:14; John 10:30
3   Hebrews 1:5–6, 8
4   John 1:14, 18
5   John 15:26; Galatians 4:6
6   Isaiah 6:3, 5, 8 compared with John 12:41 and with Acts 28:25; 1 John 5:20; Acts 5:3–4
7   John 1:1; Isaiah 9:6; John 2:24–25; 1 Corinthians 2:10–11
8   Colossians 1:16; Genesis 1:2
9   Matthew 28:19; 2 Corinthians 13:14
10 Ephesians 1:11; Romans 11:33; 9:14–15, 18
11 Ephesians 1:4, 11; Romans 9:22–23; Psalm 33:11
12 1 Timothy 5:21

to eternal life, and the means thereof:[1] and also, according to his sovereign power, and the unsearchable counsel of his own will, (whereby he extends or withholds favour as he pleases,) has passed by and foreordained the rest to dishonour and wrath, to be for their sin inflicted, to the praise of the glory of his justice.[2]

Q. 14. *How does God execute his decrees?*
A. God executes his decrees in the works of creation and providence, according to his infallible foreknowledge, and the free and immutable counsel of his own will.[3]

Q. 15. *What is the work of creation?*
A. The work of creation is that wherein God did in the beginning, by the word of his power, make of nothing the world, and all things therein, for himself, within the space of six days, and all very good.[4]

Q. 16. *How did God create angels?*
A. God created all the angels[5] spirits,[6] immortal,[7] holy,[8] excelling in knowledge,[9] mighty in power,[10] to execute his commandments, and to praise his name,[11] yet subject to change.[12]

Q. 17. *How did God create man?*
A. After God had made all other creatures, he created man male and female;[13] formed the body of the man of the dust of the ground,[14] and the woman of the rib of the man,[15] endued them with living, reasonable, and immortal souls;[16] made them after his own image,[17]

1　Ephesians 1:4–6; 2 Thessalonians 2:13–14
2　Romans 9:17–18, 21–22; Matthew 11:25–26; 2 Timothy 2:20; Jude 4; 1 Peter 2:8
3　Ephesians 1:11
4　Genesis 1; Hebrews 11:3; Proverbs 16:4
5　Colossians 1:16
6　Psalm 104:4
7　Matthew 22:30
8　Matthew 25:31
9　2 Samuel 14:17; Matthew 24:36
10　2 Thessalonians 1:7
11　Psalm 103:20–21
12　2 Peter 2:4
13　Genesis 1:27
14　Genesis 2:7
15　Genesis 2:22
16　Genesis 2:7 compared with Job 35:11 and with Ecclesiastes 12:7 and with Matthew 10:28 and with Luke 23:43
17　Genesis 1:27

in knowledge,[1] righteousness, and holiness;[2] having the law of God written in their hearts,[3] and power to fulfil it,[4] and dominion over the creatures;[5] yet subject to fall.[6]

Q. 18. *What are God's works of providence?*

A. God's works of providence are his most holy,[7] wise,[8] and powerful preserving[9] and governing[10] all his creatures; ordering them, and all their actions,[11] to his own glory.[12]

Q. 19. *What is God's providence towards the angels?*

A. God by his providence permitted some of the angels, wilfully and irrecoverably, to fall into sin and damnation,[13] limiting and ordering that, and all their sins, to his own glory;[14] and established the rest in holiness and happiness;[15] employing them all,[16] at his pleasure, in the administrations of his power, mercy, and justice.[17]

Q. 20. *What was the providence of God toward man in the estate in which he was created?*

A. The providence of God toward man in the estate in which he was created, was the placing him in paradise, appointing him to dress it, giving him liberty to eat of the fruit of the earth;[18] putting the creatures under his dominion,[19] and ordaining marriage for his help;[20] affording him communion with himself;[21] instituting the

---

1   Colossians 3:10
2   Ephesians 4:24
3   Romans 2:14–15
4   Ecclesiastes 7:29
5   Genesis 1:28
6   Genesis 3:6; Ecclesiastes 7:29
7   Psalm 145:17
8   Psalm 104:24; Isaiah 28:29
9   Hebrews 1:3
10   Psalm 103:19
11   Matthew 10:29–31; Genesis 45:7
12   Romans 11:36; Isaiah 63:14
13   Jude 6; 2 Peter 2:4; Hebrews 2:16; John 8:44
14   Job 1:12; Matthew 8:31
15   1 Timothy 5:21; Mark 8:38; Hebrews 12:22
16   Psalm 104:4
17   2 Kings 19:35; Hebrews 1:14
18   Genesis 2:8, 15–16
19   Genesis 1:28
20   Genesis 2:18
21   Genesis 1:26–29; 3:8

Sabbath;[1] entering into a covenant of life with him, upon condition of personal, perfect, and perpetual obedience,[2] of which the tree of life was a pledge;[3] and forbidding to eat of the tree of knowledge of good and evil, upon the pain of death.[4]

Q. 21. *Did man continue in that estate wherein God at first created him?*
A. Our first parents being left to the freedom of their own will, through the temptation of Satan, transgressed the commandment of God in eating the forbidden fruit; and thereby fell from the estate of innocence wherein they were created.[5]

Q. 22. *Did all mankind fall in that first transgression?*
A. The covenant being made with Adam as a public person, not for himself only, but for his posterity, all mankind descending from him by ordinary generation,[6] sinned in him, and fell with him in that first transgression.[7]

Q. 23. *Into what estate did the fall bring mankind?*
A. The fall brought mankind into an estate of sin and misery.[8]

Q. 24. *What is sin?*
A. Sin is any want of conformity unto, or transgression of, any law of God, given as a rule to the reasonable creature.[9]

Q. 25. *Wherein consists the sinfulness of that estate into which man fell?*
A. The sinfulness of that estate into which man fell, consists in the guilt of Adam's first sin,[10] the want of that righteousness wherein he was created, and the corruption of his nature, whereby he is utterly indisposed, disabled, and made opposite unto all that is spiritually good, and wholly inclined to all evil, and that continually;[11] which is commonly called original sin, and from which do proceed all actual transgressions.[12]

---

1 Genesis 2:3
2 Galatians 3:12; Romans 10:5
3 Genesis 2:9
4 Genesis 2:17
5 Genesis 3:6–8, 13; Ecclesiastes 7:29; 2 Corinthians 11:3
6 Acts 17:26
7 Genesis 2:16–17 compared with Romans 5:12–20 and with 1 Corinthians 15:21–22
8 Romans 5:12; 3:23
9 1 John 3:4; Galatians 3:10, 12
10 Romans 5:12, 19
11 Romans 3:10–19; Ephesians 2:1–3; Romans 5:6; 8:7–8; Genesis 6:5
12 James 1:14–15; Matthew 15:19

Q. 26. *How is original sin conveyed from our first parents to their posterity?*
A. Original sin is conveyed from our first parents to their posterity by natural generation, so as all that proceed from them in that way are conceived and born in sin.[1]

Q. 27. *What misery did the fall bring upon mankind?*
A. The fall brought upon mankind the loss of communion with God,[2] his displeasure and curse; so as we are by nature children of wrath,[3] bond slaves to Satan,[4] and justly liable to all punishments in this world, and that which is to come.[5]

Q. 28. *What are the punishments of sin in this world?*
A. The punishments of sin in this world are either inward, as blindness of mind,[6] a reprobate sense,[7] strong delusions,[8] hardness of heart,[9] horror of conscience,[10] and vile affections;[11] or outward, as the curse of God upon the creatures of our sakes,[12] and all other evils that befall us in our bodies, names, estates, relations, and employments;[13] together with death itself.[14]

Q. 29. *What are the punishments of sin in the world to come?*
A. The punishments of sin in the world to come, are everlasting separation from the comfortable presence of God, and most grievous torments in soul and body, without intermission, in hell-fire forever.[15]

Q. 30. *Does God leave all mankind to perish in the estate of sin and misery?*
A. God does not leave all men to perish in the estate of sin and misery,[16] into which they fell by the breach of the first covenant,

---

1 Psalm 51:5; Job 14:4; 15:14; John 3:6
2 Genesis 3:8, 10, 24
3 Ephesians 2:2–3
4 2 Timothy 2:26
5 Genesis 2:17; Lamentations 3:39; Romans 6:23; Matthew 25:41, 46; Jude 7
6 Ephesians 4:18
7 Romans 1:28
8 2 Thessalonians 2:11
9 Romans 2:5
10 Isaiah 33:14; Genesis 4:13; Matthew 27:4
11 Romans 1:26
12 Genesis 3:17
13 Deuteronomy 28:15–18
14 Romans 6:21, 23
15 2 Thessalonians 1:9; Mark 9:43, 44, 46, 48; Luke 16:24
16 1 Thessalonians 5:9

commonly called the covenant of works;[1] but of his mere love and mercy delivers his elect out of it, and brings them into an estate of salvation by the second covenant, commonly called the covenant of grace.[2]

Q. 31. *With whom was the covenant of grace made?*

A. The covenant of grace was made with Christ as the second [last] Adam, and in him with all the elect as his seed.[3]

Q. 32. *How is the grace of God manifested in the second covenant?*

A. The grace of God is manifested in the second covenant, in that he freely provides and offers to sinners a Mediator,[4] and life and salvation by him;[5] and requiring faith as the condition to interest them in him,[6] promises and gives his Holy Spirit[7] to all his elect, to work in them that faith,[8] with all other saving graces;[9] and to enable them unto all holy obedience,[10] as the evidence of the truth of their faith[11] and thankfulness to God,[12] and as the way which he has appointed them to salvation.[13]

Q. 33. *Was the covenant of grace always administered after one and the same manner?*

A. The covenant of grace was not always administered after the same manner, but the administrations of it under the Old Testament were different from those under the New.[14]

Q. 34. *How was the covenant of grace administered under the Old Testament?*

A. The covenant of grace was administered under the Old Testament,

---

1   Galatians 3:10, 12
2   Titus 3:4–7; Galatians 3:21; Romans 3:20–22
3   Galatians 3:16; Romans 5:15–21; Isaiah 53:10–11
4   Genesis 3:15; Isaiah 42:6; John 6:27
5   1 John 5:11–12
6   John 3:16; John 1:12
7   Proverbs 1:23
8   2 Corinthians 4:13
9   Galatians 5:22–23
10   Ezekiel 36:27
11   James 2:18, 22
12   2 Corinthians 5:14–15
13   Ephesians 2:18
14   2 Corinthians 3:6–9

by promises,[1] prophecies,[2] sacrifices,[3] circumcision,[4] the Passover,[5] and other types and ordinances, which did all fore-signify Christ then to come, and were for that time sufficient to build up the elect in faith in the promised Messiah,[6] by whom they then had full remission of sin, and eternal salvation.[7]

Q. 35. *How is the covenant of grace administered under the New Testament?*

A. Under the New Testament, when Christ the substance was exhibited, the same covenant of grace was and still is to be administered in the preaching of the Word,[8] and the administration of the sacraments of Baptism[9] and the Lord's Supper;[10] in which grace and salvation are held forth in more fulness, evidence, and efficacy, to all nations.[11]

Q. 36. *Who is the Mediator of the covenant of grace?*

A. The only Mediator of the covenant of grace is the Lord Jesus Christ,[12] who, being the eternal Son of God, of one substance and equal with the Father,[13] in the fullness of time became man,[14] and so was and continues to be God and man, in two entire distinct natures, and one person, forever.[15]

Q. 37. *How did Christ, being the Son of God, become man?*

A. Christ the Son of God became man, by taking to himself a true body, and a reasonable soul,[16] being conceived by the power of the Holy

---

1   Romans 15:8
2   Acts 3:20, 24
3   Hebrews 10:1
4   Romans 4:11
5   1 Corinthians 5:7
6   Hebrews 8, 9, 10; 11:13
7   Galatians 3:7–9, 14
8   Mark 16:15
9   Matthew 28:19–20
10 1 Corinthians 11:23–25
11 2 Corinthians 3:6–18; Hebrews 8:6, 10–11; Matthew 28:19
12 1 Timothy 2:5
13 John 1:1, 14; 10:30; Philippians 2:6
14 Galatians 4:4
15 Luke 1:35; Romans 9:5; Colossians 2:9; Hebrews 7:24–25
16 John 1:14; Matthew 26:38

Spirit in the womb of the virgin Mary, of her substance, and born of her,[1] yet without sin.[2]

Q. 38. *Why was it requisite that the Mediator should be God?*

A. It was requisite that the Mediator should be God, that he might sustain and keep the human nature from sinking under the infinite wrath of God, and the power of death;[3] give worth and efficacy to his sufferings, obedience, and intercession;[4] and to satisfy God's justice,[5] procure his favour,[6] purchase a peculiar people,[7] give his Spirit to them,[8] conquer all their enemies,[9] and bring them to everlasting salvation.[10]

Q. 39. *Why was it requisite that the Mediator should be man?*

A. It was requisite that the Mediator should be man, that he might advance our nature,[11] perform obedience to the law,[12] suffer and make intercession for us in our nature,[13] have a fellow-feeling of our infirmities;[14] that we might receive the adoption of sons,[15] and have comfort and access with boldness unto the throne of grace.[16]

Q. 40. *Why was it requisite that the Mediator should be God and man in one person?*

A. It was requisite that the Mediator, who was to reconcile God and man, should himself be both God and man, and this in one person, that the proper works of each nature might be accepted of God for us,[17] and relied on by us as the works of the whole person.[18]

---

1   Luke 1:27, 31, 35, 42; Galatians 4:4
2   Hebrews 4:15; Hebrews 7:26
3   Acts 2:24–25; Romans 1:4 compared with Romans 4:25; Hebrews 9:14
4   Acts 20:28; Hebrews 9:14; 7:25–28
5   Romans 3:24–26
6   Ephesians 1:16; Matthew 3:17
7   Titus 2:13–14
8   Galatians 4:6
9   Luke 1:68–69, 71, 74
10 Hebrews 5:8–9; 9:11–15
11 Hebrews 2:16
12 Galatians 4:4
13 Hebrews 2:14; 7:24–25
14 Hebrews 4:15
15 Galatians 4:5
16 Hebrews 4:16
17 Matthew 1:21, 23; 3:17; Hebrews 9:14
18 1 Peter 2:6

Q. 41. *Why was our Mediator called Jesus?*

A. Our Mediator was called Jesus, because he saves his people from their sins.[1]

Q. 42. *Why was our Mediator called Christ?*

A. Our Mediator was called Christ, because he was anointed with the Holy Spirit above measure;[2] and so set apart, and fully furnished with all authority and ability,[3] to execute the offices of prophet,[4] priest,[5] and king of his church,[6] in the estate both of his humiliation and exaltation.

Q. 43. *How does Christ execute the office of a prophet?*

A. Christ executes the office of a prophet, in his revealing to the church,[7] in all ages, by his Spirit and Word,[8] in divers [various] ways of administration,[9] the whole will of God,[10] in all things concerning their edification and salvation.[11]

Q. 44. *How does Christ execute the office of a priest?*

A. Christ executes the office of a priest, in his once offering himself a sacrifice without spot to God,[12] to be a reconciliation for the sins of his people;[13] and in making continual intercession for them.[14]

Q. 45. *How does Christ execute the office of a king?*

A. Christ executes the office of a king, in calling out of the world a people to himself,[15] and giving them officers,[16] laws,[17] and censures, by which he visibly governs them;[18] in bestowing saving grace upon

---

1 Matthew 1:21
2 John 3:34; Psalm 45:7
3 John 6:27; Matthew 28:18-20
4 Acts 3:21-22; Luke 4:18, 21
5 Hebrews 5:5-7; Hebrews 4:14-15
6 Psalm 2:6; Matthew 21:5; Isaiah 9:6-7; Philippians 2:8-11
7 John 1:18
8 1 Peter 1:10-12
9 Hebrews 1:1-2
10 John 15:15
11 Acts 20:32; Ephesians 4:11-13; John 20:31
12 Hebrews 9:14, 28
13 Hebrews 2:17
14 Hebrews 7:25
15 Acts 15:14-16; Isaiah 55:4-5; Genesis 49:10; Psalm 110:3
16 Ephesians 4:11-12; 1 Corinthians 12:28
17 Isaiah 33:22
18 Matthew 18:17-18; 1 Corinthians 5:4-5

his elect,[1] rewarding their obedience,[2] and correcting them for their sins,[3] preserving and supporting them under all their temptations and sufferings,[4] restraining and overcoming all their enemies,[5] and powerfully ordering all things for his own glory,[6] and their good;[7] and also in taking vengeance on the rest, who know not God, and obey not the gospel.[8]

Q. 46. *What was the estate of Christ's humiliation?*
A. The estate of Christ's humiliation was that low condition, wherein he for our sakes, emptying himself of his glory, took upon him the form of a servant, in his conception and birth, life, death, and after his death, until his resurrection.[9]

Q. 47. *How did Christ humble himself in his conception and birth?*
A. Christ humbled himself in his conception and birth, in that, being from all eternity the Son of God, in the bosom of the Father, he was pleased in the fullness of time to become the son of man, made of a woman of low estate, and to be born of her; with divers [various] circumstances of more than ordinary abasement.[10]

Q. 48. *How did Christ humble himself in his life?*
A. Christ humbled himself in his life, by subjecting himself to the law,[11] which he perfectly fulfilled;[12] and by conflicting with the indignities of the world,[13] temptations of Satan,[14] and infirmities in his flesh, whether common to the nature of man, or particularly accompanying that his low condition.[15]

Q. 49. *How did Christ humble himself in his death?*
A. Christ humbled himself in his death, in that having been betrayed by

---

1   Acts 5:31
2   Revelation 22:12; 2:10
3   Revelation 3:19
4   Isaiah 63:9
5   1 Corinthians 15:25; Psalm 110
6   Romans 14:10–11
7   Romans 8:28
8   2 Thessalonians 1:8–9; Psalm 2:8–9
9   Philippians 2:6–8; Luke 1:31; 2 Corinthians 8:9; Acts 2:24
10 John 1:14, 18; Galatians 4:4; Luke 2:7
11 Galatians 4:4
12 Matthew 5:17; Romans 5:19
13 Psalm 22:6; Hebrews 12:2–3
14 Matthew 4:1–12; Luke 4:13
15 Hebrews 2:17–18; 4:15; Isaiah 52:13–14

Judas,[1] forsaken by his disciples,[2] scorned and rejected by the world,[3] condemned by Pilate, and tormented by his persecutors;[4] having also conflicted with the terrors of death, and the powers of darkness, felt and borne the weight of God's wrath,[5] he laid down his life an offering for sin,[6] enduring the painful, shameful, and cursed death of the cross.[7]

Q. 50. *Wherein consisted Christ's humiliation after his death?*

A. Christ's humiliation after his death consisted in his being buried,[8] and continuing in the state of the dead, and under the power of death till the third day;[9] which has been otherwise expressed in these words, He descended into hell.

Q. 51. *What was the estate of Christ's exaltation?*

A. The estate of Christ's exaltation comprehends his resurrection,[10] ascension,[11] sitting at the right hand of the Father,[12] and his coming again to judge the world.[13]

Q. 52. *How was Christ exalted in his resurrection?*

A. Christ was exalted in his resurrection, in that, not having seen corruption in death, (of which it was not possible for him to be held,)[14] and having the very same body in which he suffered, with the essential properties thereof,[15] (but without mortality, and other common infirmities belonging to this life,) really united to his soul,[16] he rose again from the dead the third day by his own power;[17] whereby he declared himself to be the Son of God,[18] to have satisfied

---

1   Matthew 27:4
2   Matthew 26:56
3   Isaiah 53:2–3
4   Matthew 27:26–50; John 19:34
5   Luke 22:44; Matthew 27:46
6   Isaiah 53:10
7   Philippians 2:8; Hebrews 12:2; Galatians 3:13
8   1 Corinthians 15:3–4
9   Psalm 16:10 compared with Acts 2:24–27, 31; Romans 6:9; Matthew 12:40
10 1 Corinthians 15:4
11 Mark 16:19
12 Ephesians 1:20
13 Acts 1:11; 17:31
14 Acts 2:24, 27
15 Luke 24:39
16 Romans 6:9; Revelation 1:18
17 John 10:18
18 Romans 1:4

divine justice,[1] to have vanquished death, and him that had the power of it,[2] and to be Lord of quick [living] and dead:[3] all which he did as a public person,[4] the head of his church,[5] for their justification,[6] quickening in grace,[7] support against enemies,[8] and to assure them of their resurrection from the dead at the last day.[9]

Q. 53. *How was Christ exalted in his ascension?*

A. Christ was exalted in his ascension, in that having after his resurrection often appeared unto and conversed with his apostles, speaking to them of the things pertaining to the kingdom of God,[10] and giving them commission to preach the gospel to all nations,[11] forty days after his resurrection, he, in our nature, and as our head,[12] triumphing over enemies,[13] visibly went up into the highest heavens, there to receive gifts for men,[14] to raise up our affections thither,[15] and to prepare a place for us,[16] where he himself is, and shall continue till his second coming at the end of the world.[17]

Q. 54. *How is Christ exalted in his sitting at the right hand of God?*

A. Christ is exalted in his sitting at the right hand of God, in that as God-man he is advanced to the highest favour with God the Father,[18] with all fullness of joy,[19] glory,[20] and power over all things in heaven and earth;[21] and does gather and defend his church, and subdue their

---

1   Romans 8:34
2   Hebrews 2:14
3   Romans 14:9
4   1 Corinthians 15:21–22
5   Ephesians 1:20, 22, 23; Colossians 1:18
6   Romans 4:25
7   Ephesians 2:1, 5–6; Colossians 2:12
8   1 Corinthians 15:25–27
9   1 Corinthians 15:20
10 Acts 1:2–3
11 Matthew 28:19
12 Hebrews 6:20
13 Ephesians 4:8
14 Acts 1:9–11; Ephesians 4:10; Psalm 68:18
15 Colossians 3:1–2
16 John 14:3
17 Acts 3:21
18 Philippians 2:9
19 Acts 2:28 compared with Psalm 16:11
20 John 17:5
21 Ephesians 1:22; 1 Peter 3:22

enemies; furnishes his ministers and people with gifts and graces,[1] and makes intercession for them.[2]

Q. 55. *How does Christ make intercession?*

A. Christ makes intercession, by his appearing in our nature continually before the Father in heaven,[3] in the merit of his obedience and sacrifice on earth,[4] declaring his will to have it applied to all believers;[5] answering all accusations against them,[6] and procuring for them quiet of conscience, notwithstanding daily failings,[7] access with boldness to the throne of grace,[8] and acceptance of their persons[9] and services.[10]

Q. 56. *How is Christ to be exalted in his coming again to judge the world?*

A. Christ is to be exalted in his coming again to judge the world, in that he, who was unjustly judged and condemned by wicked men,[11] shall come again at the last day in great power,[12] and in the full manifestation of his own glory, and of his Father's, with all his holy angels,[13] with a shout, with the voice of the archangel, and with the trumpet of God,[14] to judge the world in righteousness.[15]

Q. 57. *What benefits has Christ procured by his mediation?*

A. Christ, by his mediation, has procured redemption,[16] with all other benefits of the covenant of grace.[17]

Q. 58. *How do we come to be made partakers of the benefits which Christ has procured?*

A. We are made partakers of the benefits which Christ has procured,

---

1 Ephesians 4:10–12; Psalm 110
2 Romans 8:34
3 Hebrews 9:12, 24
4 Hebrews 1:3
5 John 3:16; 17:9, 20, 24
6 Romans 8:33–34
7 Romans 5:1–2; 1 John 2:1–2
8 Hebrews 4:16
9 Ephesians 1:6
10 1 Peter 2:5
11 Acts 3:14–15
12 Matthew 24:30
13 Luke 9:26; Matthew 25:31
14 1 Thessalonians 4:16
15 Acts 17:31
16 Hebrews 9:12
17 2 Corinthians 1:20

by the application of them unto us,[1] which is the work especially of God the Holy Spirit.[2]

Q. 59. *Who are made partakers of redemption through Christ?*

A. Redemption is certainly applied, and effectually communicated, to all those for whom Christ has purchased it;[3] who are in time by the Holy Spirit enabled to believe in Christ according to the gospel.[4]

Q. 60. *Can they who have never heard the gospel, and so know not Jesus Christ, nor believe in him, be saved by their living according to the light of nature?*

A. They who, having never heard the gospel,[5] know not Jesus Christ,[6] and believe not in him, cannot be saved,[7] be they never so diligent to frame their lives according to the light of nature,[8] or the laws of that religion which they profess;[9] neither is there salvation in any other, but in Christ alone,[10] who is the Saviour only of his body the church.[11]

Q. 61. *Are all they saved who hear the gospel, and live in the church?*

A. All that hear the gospel, and live in the visible church, are not saved; but they only who are true members of the church invisible.[12]

Q. 62. *What is the visible church?*

A. The visible church is a society made up of all such as in all ages and places of the world do profess the true religion,[13] and of their children.[14]

Q. 63. *What are the special privileges of the visible church?*

A. The visible church has the privilege of being under God's special

---

1   John 1:11–12
2   Titus 3:5–6
3   Ephesians 1:13–14; John 6:37, 39; 10:15–16
4   Ephesians 2:8; 2 Corinthians 4:13
5   Romans 10:14
6   2 Thessalonians 1:8–9; Ephesians 2:12; John 1:10–12
7   John 8:24; Mark 16:16
8   1 Corinthians 1:20–24
9   John 4:22; Romans 9:31–32; Philippians 3:4–9
10   Acts 4:12
11   Ephesians 5:23
12   John 12:38–40; Romans 9:6; 22:14; Matthew 7:21; Romans 11:7
13   1 Corinthians 1:2; 12:13; Romans 15:9–12; Revelation 7:9; Psalm 2:8; 22:27–31; 45:17; Matthew 28:19–20; Isaiah 59:21
14   1 Corinthians 7:14; Acts 2:39; Romans 11:16; Genesis 17:7

care and government;[1] of being protected and preserved in all ages, notwithstanding the opposition of all enemies;[2] and of enjoying the communion of saints, the ordinary means of salvation,[3] and offers of grace by Christ to all the members of it in the ministry of the gospel, testifying, that whosoever believes in him shall be saved,[4] and excluding none that will come unto him.[5]

Q. 64. *What is the invisible church?*

A. The invisible church is the whole number of the elect, that have been, are, or shall be gathered into one under Christ the head.[6]

Q. 65. *What special benefits do the members of the invisible church enjoy by Christ?*

A. The members of the invisible church by Christ enjoy union and communion with him in grace and glory.[7]

Q. 66. *What is that union which the elect have with Christ?*

A. The union which the elect have with Christ is the work of God's grace,[8] whereby they are spiritually and mystically, yet really and inseparably, joined to Christ as their head and husband;[9] which is done in their effectual calling.[10]

Q. 67. *What is effectual calling?*

A. Effectual calling is the work of God's almighty power and grace,[11] whereby (out of his free and special love to his elect, and from nothing in them moving him thereunto)[12] he does, in his accepted time, invite and draw them to Jesus Christ, by his Word and Spirit;[13] savingly enlightening their minds,[14] renewing and powerfully determining their wills,[15] so as they (although in themselves dead in

---

1 Isaiah 9:5-6; 1 Timothy 4:10
2 Psalm 115; Isaiah 31:4-5; Zechariah 12:2-4, 8-9
3 Acts 2:39, 42
4 Psalm 147:19-20; Romans 9:4; Ephesians 4:11-12; Mark 16:15-16
5 John 6:37
6 Ephesians 1:10, 22-23; John 10:16; 11:52
7 John 17:21; Ephesians 2:5-6; John 17:24
8 Ephesians 1:22; 2:6-8
9 1 Corinthians 6:17; John 10:28; Ephesians 5:23, 30
10 1 Peter 5:10, 1 Corinthians 1:9
11 John 5:25; Ephesians 1:18-20; 2 Timothy 1:8-9
12 Titus 3:4-5; Ephesians 2:4-5, 7-9; Romans 9:11
13 2 Corinthians 5:20 compared with 2 Corinthians 6:1-2; John 6:44; 2 Thessalonians 2:13-14
14 Acts 26:18; 1 Corinthians 2:10, 12
15 Ezekiel 11:19; 36:26; John 6:45

sin) are hereby made willing and able freely to answer his call, and to accept and embrace the grace offered and conveyed therein.[1]

Q. 68. *Are the elect only effectually called?*

A. All the elect, and they only, are effectually called:[2] although others may be, and often are, outwardly called by the ministry of the Word,[3] and have some common operations of the Spirit;[4] who, for their wilful neglect and contempt of the grace offered to them, being justly left in their unbelief, do never truly come to Jesus Christ.[5]

Q. 69. *What is the communion in grace which the members of the invisible church have with Christ?*

A. The communion in grace which the members of the invisible church have with Christ, is their partaking of the virtue of his mediation, in their justification,[6] adoption,[7] sanctification, and whatever else, in this life, manifests their union with him.[8]

Q. 70. *What is justification?*

A. Justification is an act of God's free grace unto sinners,[9] in which he pardons all their sins, accepts and accounts their persons righteous in his sight;[10] not for anything wrought in them, or done by them,[11] but only for the perfect obedience and full satisfaction of Christ, by God imputed to them,[12] and received by faith alone.[13]

Q. 71. *How is justification an act of God's free grace?*

A. Although Christ, by his obedience and death, did make a proper, real, and full satisfaction to God's justice in the behalf of them that are justified;[14] yet in as much as God accepts the satisfaction from a surety, which he might have demanded of them, and did

---

1   Ephesians 2:5; Philippians 2:13; Deuteronomy 30:6
2   Acts 13:48
3   Matthew 22:14
4   Matthew 7:22; 13:20–21; Hebrews 6:4–6
5   John 12:38–40; Acts 28:25–27; John 6:64–65; Psalm 81:11–12
6   Romans 8:30
7   Ephesians 1:5
8   1 Corinthians 1:30
9   Romans 3:22, 24–25; Romans 4:5
10   2 Corinthians 5:19, 21; Romans 3:22, 24–25, 27–28
11   Titus 3:5, 7; Ephesians 1:7
12   Romans 5:17–19; 4:6–8
13   Acts 10:43; Galatians 2:16; Philippians 3:9
14   Romans 5:8–10, 19

provide this surety, his own only Son,[1] imputing his righteousness to them,[2] and requiring nothing of them for their justification but faith,[3] which also is his gift,[4] their justification is to them of free grace.[5]

Q. 72. *What is justifying faith?*
A. Justifying faith is a saving grace,[6] wrought in the heart of a sinner by the Spirit[7] and Word of God,[8] whereby he, being convinced of his sin and misery, and of the disability in himself and all other creatures to recover him out of his lost condition,[9] not only assents to the truth of the promise of the gospel,[10] but receives and rests upon Christ and his righteousness, therein held forth, for pardon of sin,[11] and for the accepting and accounting of his person righteous in the sight of God for salvation.[12]

Q. 73. *How does faith justify a sinner in the sight of God?*
A. Faith justifies a sinner in the sight of God, not because of those other graces which do always accompany it, or of good works that are the fruits of it,[13] nor as if the grace of faith, or any act thereof, were imputed to him for his justification;[14] but only as it is an instrument by which he receives and applies Christ and his righteousness.[15]

Q. 74. *What is adoption?*
A. Adoption is an act of the free grace of God,[16] in and for his only Son Jesus Christ,[17] whereby all those that are justified are received into

---

1 1 Timothy 2:5-6; Hebrews 10:10; Matthew 20:28; Daniel 9:24, 26; Isaiah 53:4-6, 10-12; Hebrews 7:22; Romans 8:32; 1 Peter 1:18-19
2 2 Corinthians 5:21
3 Romans 3:24-25
4 Ephesians 2:8
5 Ephesians 1:7
6 Hebrews 10:39
7 2 Corinthians 4:13; Ephesians 1:17-19
8 Romans 10:14, 17
9 Acts 2:37; 16:30; John 16:8-9; Romans 6:6; Ephesians 2:1; Acts 4:12
10 Ephesians 1:13
11 John 1:12; Acts 16:31; 10:43
12 Philippians 3:9; Acts 15:11
13 Galatians 3:11; Romans 3:28
14 Romans 4:5 compared with Romans 10:10
15 John 1:12; Philippians 3:9; Galatians 1:16
16 1 John 3:1
17 Ephesians 1:5; Galatians 4:4-5

the number of his children,[1] have his name put upon them,[2] the Spirit of his Son given to them,[3] are under his fatherly care and dispensations,[4] admitted to all the liberties and privileges of the sons of God, made heirs of all the promises, and fellow-heirs with Christ in glory.[5]

Q. 75. *What is sanctification?*

A. Sanctification is a work of God's grace, whereby they whom God has, before the foundation of the world, chosen to be holy, are in time, through the powerful operation of his Spirit[6] applying the death and resurrection of Christ unto them,[7] renewed in their whole man after the image of God;[8] having the seeds of repentance unto life, and all other saving graces, put into their hearts,[9] and those graces so stirred up, increased, and strengthened,[10] as that they more and more die unto sin, and rise unto newness of life.[11]

Q. 76. *What is repentance unto life?*

A. Repentance unto life is a saving grace,[12] wrought in the heart of a sinner by the Spirit[13] and Word of God,[14] whereby, out of the sight and sense, not only of the danger,[15] but also of the filthiness and odiousness of his sins,[16] and upon the apprehension of God's mercy in Christ to such as are penitent,[17] he so grieves for[18] and hates his sins,[19] as that he turns from them all to God,[20] purposing and

---

1   John 1:12
2   2 Corinthians 6:18; Revelation 3:12
3   Galatians 4:6
4   Psalm 103:13; Proverbs 14:26; Matthew 6:32
5   Hebrews 6:12; Romans 8:17
6   Ephesians 1:4; 1 Corinthians 6:11; 2 Thessalonians 2:13
7   Romans 6:4–6
8   Ephesians 4:23–24
9   Acts 11:18; 1 John 3:9
10 Jude 20; Hebrews 6:11–12; Ephesians 3:16–19; Colossians 1:10–11
11 Romans 6:4, 6, 14; Galatians 5:24
12 2 Timothy 2:25
13 Zechariah 12:10
14 Acts 11:18, 20–21
15 Ezekiel 18:28.3 0, 32; Luke 15:17–18; Hosea 2:6–7
16 Ezekiel 36:31; Isaiah 30:22
17 Joel 2:12–13
18 Jeremiah 31:18–19
19 2 Corinthians 7:11
20 Acts 26:18; Ezekiel 14:6; 1 Kings 8:47–48

endeavouring constantly to walk with him in all the ways of new obedience.[1]

Q. 77. *Wherein do justification and sanctification differ?*

A. Although sanctification be inseparably joined with justification,[2] yet they differ, in that God in justification imputes the righteousness of Christ;[3] in sanctification his Spirit infuses grace, and enables to the exercise thereof;[4] in the former, sin is pardoned;[5] in the other, it is subdued:[6] the one does equally free all believers from the revenging wrath of God, and that perfectly in this life, that they never fall into condemnation;[7] the other is neither equal in all,[8] nor in this life perfect in any,[9] but growing up to perfection.[10]

Q. 78. *Whence arises the imperfection of sanctification in believers?*

A. The imperfection of sanctification in believers arises from the remnants of sin abiding in every part of them, and the perpetual lusting of the flesh against the spirit; whereby they are often foiled with temptations, and fall into many sins,[11] are hindered in all their spiritual services,[12] and their best works are imperfect and defiled in the sight of God.[13]

Q. 79. *May not true believers, by reason of their imperfections, and the many temptations and sins they are overtaken with, fall away from the state of grace?*

A. True believers, by reason of the unchangeable love of God,[14] and his decree and covenant to give them perseverance,[15] their inseparable union with Christ,[16] his continual intercession for them,[17] and the

---

1   Psalm 119:6 ,59, 128; Luke 1:6; 2 Kings 23:25
2   1 Corinthians 6:11; 1 Corinthians 1:30
3   Romans 4:6, 8
4   Ezekiel 36:27
5   Romans 3:24-25
6   Romans 6:6, 14
7   Romans 8:33-34
8   1 John 2:12-14; Hebrews 5:12-14
9   1 John 1:8, 10
10 2 Corinthians 7:1; Philippians 3:12-14
11 Romans 7:18, 23; Mark 14:66-72; Galatians 2:11-12
12 Hebrew 12:1
13 Isaiah 64:6; Exodus 28:38
14 Jeremiah 31:3
15 2 Timothy 2:19; Hebrews 13:20-21; 2 Samuel 23:5
16 1 Corinthians 1:8-9
17 Hebrews 7:25; Luke 22:32

Spirit and seed of God abiding in them,[1] can neither totally nor finally fall away from the state of grace,[2] but are kept by the power of God through faith unto salvation.[3]

Q. 80. *Can true believers be infallibly assured that they are in the estate of grace, and that they shall persevere therein unto salvation?*

A. Such as truly believe in Christ, and endeavour to walk in all good conscience before him,[4] may, without extraordinary revelation, by faith grounded upon the truth of God's promises, and by the Spirit enabling them to discern in themselves those graces to which the promises of life are made,[5] and bearing witness with their spirits that they are the children of God,[6] be infallibly assured that they are in the estate of grace, and shall persevere therein unto salvation.[7]

Q. 81. *Are all true believers at all times assured of their present being in the estate of grace, and that they shall be saved?*

A. Assurance of grace and salvation not being of the essence of faith,[8] true believers may wait long before they obtain it;[9] and, after the enjoyment thereof, may have it weakened and intermitted, through manifold distempers [afflictions], sins, temptations, and desertions;[10] yet they are never left without such a presence and support of the Spirit of God as keeps them from sinking into utter despair.[11]

Q. 82. *What is the communion in glory which the members of the invisible church have with Christ?*

A. The communion in glory which the members of the invisible church

---

1   1 John 3:9; 1 John 2:27
2   Jeremiah 32:40; John 10:28
3   1 Peter 1:5
4   1 John 2:3
5   1 Corinthians 2:12; 1 John 3:14, 18–19, 21, 24; 4:13, 16; Hebrews 6:11–12
6   Romans 8:16
7   1 John 5:13
8   Ephesians 1:13
9   Isaiah 50:10; Psalm 88
10 Psalm 77:1–12; Song of Solomon 5:2–3, 6; Psalm 51:8; 31:22; 22:1
11 1 John 3:9; Job 13:15; Psalm 73:15, 23; Isaiah 54:7–10

have with Christ, is in this life,[1] immediately after death,[2] and at last perfected at the resurrection and day of judgment.[3]

Q. 83. *What is the communion in glory with Christ which the members of the invisible church enjoy in this life?*

A. The members of the invisible church have communicated to them in this life the firstfruits of glory with Christ, as they are members of him their head, and so in him are interested in that glory which he is fully possessed of;[4] and, as an earnest [pledge] thereof, enjoy the sense of God's love,[5] peace of conscience, joy in the Holy Spirit, and hope of glory;[6] as, on the contrary, sense of God's revenging wrath, horror of conscience, and a fearful expectation of judgment, are to the wicked the beginning of their torments which they shall endure after death.[7]

Q. 84. *Shall all men die?*

A. Death being threatened as the wages of sin,[8] it is appointed unto all men once to die;[9] for that all have sinned.[10]

Q. 85. *Death, being the wages of sin, why are not the righteous delivered from death, seeing all their sins are forgiven in Christ?*

A. The righteous shall be delivered from death itself at the last day, and even in death are delivered from the sting and curse of it;[11] so that, although they die, yet it is out of God's love,[12] to free them perfectly from sin and misery,[13] and to make them capable of further communion with Christ in glory, which they then enter upon.[14]

Q. 86. *What is the communion in glory with Christ, which the members of the invisible church enjoy immediately after death?*

A. The communion in glory, which the members of the

---

1   2 Corinthians 3:18
2   Luke 23:43
3   1 Thessalonians 4:17
4   Ephesians 2:5–6
5   Romans 5:5; 2 Corinthians 1:22
6   Romans 5:1–2; 14:17
7   Genesis 4:13; Matthew 27:4; Hebrews 10:27; Romans 2:9; Mark 9:44
8   Romans 6:23
9   Hebrews 9:27
10 Romans 5:12
11 1 Corinthians 15:26, 55–57; Hebrews 2:15
12 Isaiah 57:1–2; 2 Kings 22:20
13 Revelation 14:13; Ephesians 5:27
14 Luke 23:43; Philippians 1:23

invisible church enjoy immediately after death is, in that their souls are then made perfect in holiness,[1] and received into the highest heavens,[2] where they behold the face of God in light and glory,[3] waiting for the full redemption of their bodies,[4] which even in death continue united to Christ,[5] and rest in their graves as in their beds,[6] till at the last day they be again united to their souls.[7] Whereas the souls of the wicked are at their death cast into hell, where they remain in torments and utter darkness, and their bodies kept in their graves, as in their prisons, till the resurrection and judgment of the great day.[8]

Q. 87. *What are we to believe concerning the resurrection?*
A. We are to believe that at the last day there shall be a general resurrection of the dead, both of the just and unjust:[9] when they that are then found alive shall in a moment be changed; and the self-same bodies of the dead which were laid in the grave, being then again united to their souls forever, shall be raised up by the power of Christ.[10] The bodies of the just, by the Spirit of Christ, and by virtue of his resurrection as their head, shall be raised in power, spiritual, incorruptible, and made like to his glorious body;[11] and the bodies of the wicked shall be raised up in dishonour by him, as an offended judge.[12]

Q. 88. *What shall immediately follow after the resurrection?*
A. Immediately after the resurrection shall follow the general and final judgment of angels and men;[13] the day and hour whereof no man knows, that all may watch and pray, and be ever ready for the coming of the Lord.[14]

---

1   Hebrews 12:23
2   2 Corinthians 5:1, 6, 8; Philippians 1:23 compared with Acts 3:21 and with Ephesians 4:10
3   1 John 3:2; 1 Corinthians 13:12
4   Romans 8:23; Psalm 16:9
5   1 Thessalonians 4:14
6   Isaiah 57:2
7   Job 19:26-27
8   Luke 16:23-24; Acts 1:25; Jude 6-7
9   Acts 24:15
10   1 Corinthians 15:51-53; 1 Thessalonians 4:15-17; John 5:28-29
11   1 Corinthians 15:21-23, 42-44; Philippians 3:21
12   John 5:27-29; Matthew 25:33
13   2 Peter 2:4; Jude 6-7, 14-15; Matthew 25:46
14   Matthew 24:36, 42, 44; Luke 21:35-36

Q. 89. *What shall be done to the wicked at the day of judgment?*

A. At the day of judgment, the wicked shall be set on Christ's left hand,[1] and, upon clear evidence, and full conviction of their own consciences,[2] shall have the fearful but just sentence of condemnation pronounced against them;[3] and thereupon shall be cast out from the favourable presence of God, and the glorious fellowship with Christ, his saints, and all his holy angels, into hell, to be punished with unspeakable torments, both of body and soul, with the devil and his angels forever.[4]

Q. 90. *What shall be done to the righteous at the day of judgment?*

A. At the day of judgment, the righteous, being caught up to Christ in the clouds,[5] shall be set on his right hand, and there openly acknowledged and acquitted,[6] shall join with him in the judging of reprobate angels and men,[7] and shall be received into heaven,[8] where they shall be fully and forever freed from all sin and misery;[9] filled with inconceivable joys,[10] made perfectly holy and happy both in body and soul, in the company of innumerable saints and holy angels,[11] but especially in the immediate vision and fruition of God the Father, of our Lord Jesus Christ, and of the Holy Spirit, to all eternity.[12] And this is the perfect and full communion, which the members of the invisible church shall enjoy with Christ in glory, at the resurrection and day of judgment.

---

1   Matthew 25:33
2   Romans 2:15–16
3   Matthew 25:41–43
4   Luke 16:26; 2 Thessalonians 1:8–9
5   1 Thessalonians 4:17
6   Matthew 25:33; 10:32
7   1 Corinthians 6:2–3
8   Matthew 25:34, 46
9   Ephesians 5:27; Revelation 14:13
10 Psalm 16:11
11 Hebrews 12:22–23
12 1 John 3:2; 1 Corinthians 13:12; 1 Thessalonians 4:17–18

Having Seen What the Scriptures Principally Teach Us To Believe Concerning God, It Follows to Consider What They Require as the Duty of Man

Q. 91. *What is the duty which God requires of man?*
A. The duty which God requires of man, is obedience to his revealed will.[1]

Q. 92. *What did God at first reveal unto man as the rule of his obedience?*
A. The rule of obedience revealed to Adam in the estate of innocence, and to all mankind in him, besides a special command not to eat of the fruit of the tree knowledge of good and evil, was the moral law.[2]

Q. 93. *What is the moral law?*
A. The moral law is the declaration of the will of God to mankind, directing and binding everyone to personal, perfect, and perpetual conformity and obedience thereunto, in the frame and disposition of the whole man, soul and body,[3] and in performance of all those duties of holiness and righteousness which he owes to God and man:[4] promising life upon the fulfilling, and threatening death upon the breach of it.[5]

Q. 94. *Is there any use of the moral law to man since the fall?*
A. Although no man, since the fall, can attain to righteousness and life by the moral law:[6] yet there is great use thereof, as well common to all men, as peculiar either to the unregenerate, or the regenerate.[7]

Q. 95. *Of what use is the moral law to all men?*
A. The moral law is of use to all men, to inform them of the holy nature and the will of God,[8] and of their duty, binding them to walk accordingly;[9] to convince them of their disability to keep it, and of

---

1 Romans 12:1–2; Micah 6:8; 1 Samuel 15:22
2 Genesis 1:26–27; Romans 2:14–15; 10:5; Genesis 2:17
3 Deuteronomy 5:1–3, 31, 33; Luke 10:26–27; 1 Thessalonians 5:23
4 Luke 1:75; Acts 24:16
5 Romans 10:5; Galatians 3:10, 12
6 Romans 8:3; Galatians 2:16
7 1 Timothy 1:8
8 Leviticus 11:44–45; Leviticus 20:7–8; Romans 8:12
9 Micah 6:8; James 2:10–11

the sinful pollution of their nature, hearts, and lives:[1] to humble them in the sense of their sin and misery,[2] and thereby help them to a clearer sight of the need they have of Christ,[3] and of the perfection of his obedience.[4]

Q. 96. *What particular use is there of the moral law to unregenerate men?*

A. The moral law is of use to unregenerate men, to awaken their consciences to flee from wrath to come,[5] and to drive them to Christ;[6] or, upon their continuance in the estate and way of sin, to leave them inexcusable,[7] and under the curse thereof.[8]

Q. 97. *What special use is there of the moral law to the regenerate?*

A. Although they that are regenerate, and believe in Christ, be delivered from the moral law as a covenant of works,[9] so as thereby they are neither justified[10] nor condemned;[11] yet, besides the general uses thereof common to them with all men, it is of special use, to show them how much they are bound to Christ for his fulfilling it, and enduring the curse thereof in their stead, and for their good;[12] and thereby to provoke them to more thankfulness,[13] and to express the same in their greater care to conform themselves thereunto as the rule of their obedience.[14]

Q. 98. *Where is the moral law summarily comprehended?*

A. The moral law is summarily comprehended in the ten commandments, which were delivered by the voice of God upon Mount Sinai, and written by him in two tables of stone;[15] and are recorded in the twentieth chapter of Exodus. The four first

---

1   Psalm 19:11-12; Romans 3:20; 7:7
2   Romans 3:9, 23
3   Galatians 3:21-22
4   Romans 10:4
5   1 Timothy 1:9-10
6   Galatians 3:24
7   Romans 1:20 compared with Romans 2:15
8   Galatians 3:10
9   Romans 6:14; 7:4, 6; Galatians 4:4-5
10 Romans 3:20
11 Galatians 5:23; Romans 8:1
12 Romans 7:24-25; Galatians 3:13-14; Romans 8:3-4
13 Luke 1:68-69, 74-75; Colossians 1:12-14
14 Romans 7:22; 12:2; Titus 2:11-14
15 Deuteronomy 10:4; Exodus 34:1-4

commandments containing our duty to God, and the other six our duty to man.[1]

Q. 99. *What rules are to be observed for the right understanding of the Ten Commandments?*

A. For the right understanding of the Ten Commandments, these rules are to be observed:

1. That the law is perfect, and binds everyone to full conformity in the whole man unto the righteousness thereof, and unto entire obedience forever; so as to require the utmost perfection of every duty, and to forbid the least degree of every sin.[2]

2. That it is spiritual, and so reaches the understanding, will, affections, and all other powers of the soul; as well as words, works, and gestures.[3]

3. That one and the same thing, in divers [various] respects, is required or forbidden in several commandments.[4]

4. That as, where a duty is commanded, the contrary sin is forbidden;[5] and, where a sin is forbidden, the contrary duty is commanded:[6] so, where a promise is annexed, the contrary threatening is included;[7] and, where a threatening is annexed, the contrary promise is included.[8]

5. That what God forbids, is at no time to be done;[9] what he commands, is always our duty;[10] and yet every particular duty is not to be done at all times.[11]

6. That under one sin or duty, all of the same kind are forbidden or commanded; together with all the causes, means, occasions, and appearances thereof, and provocations thereunto.[12]

7. That what is forbidden or commanded to ourselves, we are bound,

---

1   Matthew 22:37–40
2   Psalm 19:7; James 2:10; Matthew 5:21–22
3   Romans 7:14; Deuteronomy 6:5 compared with Matthew 22:37–39; Matthew 5:21–22, 27–28, 33–34, 37–39, 43–44
4   Colossians 3:5; Amos 8:5; Proverbs 1:19; 1 Timothy 6:10
5   Isaiah 58:13; Deuteronomy 6:13 compared with Matthew 4:9–10; Matthew 15:4–6
6   Matthew 5:21–25; Ephesians 4:28
7   Exodus 20:12 compared with Proverbs 30:17
8   Jeremiah 18:7–8 compared with Psalm 15:1, 4–5 and with Psalm 24:4–5; Exodus 20:7
9   Job 13:7–8; Romans 3:8; Job 36:21
10   Deuteronomy 4:8–9
11   Matthew 12:7
12   Matthew 5:21–22, 27–28; 15:4–6; Hebrews 10:24–25; 1 Thessalonians 5:22; Jude 23; Galatians 5:26; Colossians 3:21

according to our places to endeavour that it may be avoided or performed by others, according to the duty of their places.[1]

8. That in what is commanded to others, we are bound, according to our places and callings, to be helpful to them;[2] and to take heed of partaking with others in what is forbidden them.[3]

Q. 100. *What special things are we to consider in the Ten Commandments?*

A. We are to consider in the Ten Commandments, the preface, the substance of the commandments themselves, and several reasons annexed to some of them, the more to enforce them.

Q. 101. *What is the preface to the Ten Commandments?*

A. The preface to the Ten Commandments is contained in these words, I am the Lord your God, who has brought you out of the land of Egypt, out of the house of slavery.[4] Wherein God manifests his sovereignty, as being JEHOVAH [covenant Lord], the eternal, immutable, and almighty God;[5] having his being in and of himself,[6] and giving being to all his words[7] and works:[8] and that he is a God in covenant, as with Israel of old, so with all his people;[9] who, as he brought them out of their bondage in Egypt, so he delivers us from our spiritual thraldom [captivity];[10] and that therefore we are bound to take him for our God alone, and to keep all his commandments.[11]

Q. 102. *What is the sum of the four commandments which contain our duty to God?*

A. The sum of the four commandments containing our duty to God is, to love the Lord our God with all our heart, and with all our soul, and with all our strength, and with all our mind.[12]

Q. 103. *Which is the first commandment?*

A. The first commandment is, You shall have no other gods before me.[13]

---

1   Exodus 20:10; Leviticus 19:17; Genesis 18:19; Joshua 14:15; Deuteronomy 6:6–7
2   2 Corinthians 1:24
3   1 Timothy 5:22; Ephesians 5:11
4   Exodus 20:2
5   Isaiah 44:6
6   Exodus 3:14
7   Exodus 6:3
8   Acts 17:24, 28
9   Genesis 17:7 compared with Romans 3:29
10 Luke 1:74–75
11 1 Peter 1:15, 17–18; Leviticus 18:30; 19:37
12 Luke 10:27
13 Exodus 20:3

Q. 104. *What are the duties required in the first commandment?*

A. The duties required in the first commandment are, the knowing and acknowledging of God to be the only true God, and our God;[1] and to worship and glorify him accordingly,[2] by thinking,[3] meditating,[4] remembering,[5] highly esteeming,[6] honouring,[7] adoring,[8] choosing,[9] loving,[10] desiring,[11] fearingof him;[12] believing him;[13] trusting[14] hoping,[15] delighting,[16] rejoicing in him;[17] being zealous for him;[18] calling upon him, giving all praise and thanks,[19] and yielding all obedience and submission to him with the whole man;[20] being careful in all things to please him,[21] and sorrowful when in anything he is offended;[22] and walking humbly with him.[23]

Q. 105. *What are the sins forbidden in the first commandment?*

A. The sins forbidden in the first commandment are, atheism, in denying or not having a God;[24] idolatry, in having or worshipping more gods than one, or any with or instead of the true God;[25] the not having and avouching him for God, and our God;[26] the omission or neglect of anything due to him, required in this commandment;[27]

---

1   1 Chronicles 28:9; Deuteronomy 26:7; Isaiah 43:10; Jeremiah 14:22
2   Psalm 95:6–7; Matthew 4:10; Psalm 29:2
3   Malachi 3:16
4   Psalm 63:6
5   Ecclesiastes 12:1
6   Psalm 71:19
7   Malachi 1:6
8   Isaiah 45:23
9   Joshua 24:15, 22
10 Deuteronomy 6:5
11 Psalm 73:25
12 Isaiah 8:13
13 Exodus 14:31
14 Isaiah 26:4
15 Psalm 130:7
16 Psalm 37:4
17 Psalm 32:11
18 Romans 12:11 compared with Numbers 25:11
19 Philippians 4:6
20 Jeremiah 7:23; James 4:7
21 1 John 3:22
22 Jeremiah 31:18; Psalm 119:136
23 Micah 6:8
24 Psalm 14:1; Ephesians 2:12
25 Jeremiah 2:27, 28 compared with 1 Thessalonians 1:9
26 Psalm 81:11
27 Isaiah 43:2, 23–24

ignorance,[1] forget-fullness,[2] misapprehensions,[3] false opinions,[4] unworthy and wicked thoughts of him;[5] bold and curious searching into his secrets;[6] all profaneness,[7] hatred of God;[8] self-love,[9] self-seeking,[10] and all other inordinate and immoderate setting of our mind, will, or affections upon other things, and taking them off from him in whole or in part;[11] vain credulity,[12] unbelief,[13] heresy,[14] misbelief,[15] distrust,[16] despair,[17] incorrigibleness,[18] and insensibleness under judgments,[19] hardness of heart,[20] pride,[21] presumption,[22] carnal security,[23] tempting of God;[24] using unlawful means,[25] and trusting in lawful means;[26] carnal delights and joys;[27] corrupt, blind, and indiscreet zeal;[28] lukewarmness,[29] and deadness in the things of God;[30] estranging ourselves, and apostatizing from God;[31] praying, or giving any religious worship, to saints, angels, or any other creatures;[32] all compacts and consulting with the

1   Jeremiah 4:22; Hosea 4:1, 6
2   Jeremiah 2:32
3   Acts 17:23, 29
4   Isaiah 40:18
5   Psalm 50:21
6   Deuteronomy 29:29
7   Titus 1:16; Hebrews 12:16
8   Romans 1:30
9   2 Timothy 3:2
10 Philippians 2:21
11 1 John 2:15–16; 1 Samuel 2:29; Colossians 2:2, 5
12 1 John 4:1
13 Hebrews 3:12
14 Galatians 5:20; Titus 3:10
15 Acts 26:9
16 Psalm 78:22
17 Genesis 4:13
18 Jeremiah 5:3
19 Isaiah 42:25
20 Romans 2:5
21 Jeremiah 13:15
22 Psalm 10:13
23 Zephaniah 1:12
24 Matthew 4:7
25 Romans 3:8
26 Jeremiah 17:5
27 2 Timothy 3:4
28 Galatians 4:17; John 16:2; Romans 10:2; Luke 9:54–55
29 Revelation 3:16
30 Revelation 2:1
31 Ezekiel 14:5; Isaiah 1:4–5
32 Romans 10:13–14; Hosea 4:12; Acts 10:25–26; Revelation 19:10; Matthew 4:10; Colossians 2:18; Romans 1:25

devil,[1] and hearkening to his suggestions;[2] making men the lords of our faith and conscience;[3] slighting and despising God and his commands;[4] resisting and grieving of his Spirit,[5] discontent and impatience at his dispensations, charging him foolishly for the evils he inflicts on us;[6] and ascribing the praise of any good we either are, have or can do, to fortune,[7] idols,[8] ourselves,[9] or any other creature.[10]

Q. 106. *What are we specially taught by these words before me in the first commandment?*

A. These words before me or before my face, in the first commandment, teach us, that God, who sees all things, takes special notice of, and is much displeased with, the sin of having any other God: that so it may be an argument to dissuade from it, and to aggravate it as a most impudent provocation:[11] as also to persuade us to do as in his sight, whatever we do in his service.[12]

Q. 107. *Which is the second commandment?*

A. The second commandment is, You shall not make for yourself a carved image, or any likeness of anything that is in heaven above, or that is in the earth beneath, or that is in the water under the earth. You shall not bow down to them or serve them: for I the Lord your God am a jealous God, visiting the iniquity of the fathers upon the children to the third and fourth generation of those who hate me; and showing steadfast love to thousands of those who love me, and keep my commandments.[13]

Q. 108. *What are the duties required in the second commandment?*

A. The duties required in the second commandment are, the receiving, observing, and keeping pure and entire, all such religious worship

---

1   Leviticus 20:6; 1 Samuel 28:7, 11 compared with 1 Chronicles 10:13–14
2   Acts 5:3
3   2 Corinthians 1:24; Matthew 23:9
4   Deuteronomy 32:15; 2 Samuel 12:9; Proverbs 13:13
5   Acts 7:51; Ephesians 4:30
6   Psalm 73:2–3, 13–15, 22; Job 1:22
7   1 Samuel 6:7–9
8   Daniel 5:23
9   Deuteronomy 8:17; Daniel 4:30
10   Habakkuk 1:16
11   Ezekiel 8:5–6; Psalm 44:20–21
12   1 Chronicles 28:9
13   Exodus 20:4–6

and ordinances as God has instituted in his Word;[1] particularly prayer and thanksgiving in the name of Christ;[2] the reading, preaching, and hearing of the Word;[3] the administration and receiving of the sacraments;[4] church government and discipline;[5] the ministry and maintenance thereof;[6] religious fasting;[7] swearing by the name of God,[8] and vowing unto him:[9] as also the disapproving, detesting, opposing all false worship;[10] and, according to each one's place and calling, removing it, and all monuments of idolatry.[11]

Q. 109. *What are the sins forbidden in the second commandment?*
A. The sins forbidden in the second commandment are, all devising,[12] counselling,[13] commanding,[14] using,[15] and anywise approving, any religious worship not instituted by God himself;[16] tolerating a false religion; the making any representation of God, of all or of any of the three persons, either inwardly in our mind, or outwardly in any kind of image or likeness of any creature whatsoever;[17] all worshipping of it,[18] or God in it or by it;[19] the making of any representation of feigned deities,[20] and all worship of them, or service belonging to them;[21] all superstitious devices,[22] corrupting the worship of God,[23] adding to it, or taking from it,[24] whether

1 Deuteronomy 32:46–47; Matthew 28:20; Acts 2:42; 1 Timothy 6:13–14
2 Philippians 4:6; Ephesians 5:20
3 Deuteronomy 17:18–19; Acts 15:21; 2 Timothy 4:2; James 1:21–22; Acts 10:33
4 Matthew 28:19; 1 Corinthians 11:23–30
5 Matthew 18:15–17; 16:19; 1 Corinthians 5; 12:28
6 Ephesians 4:11–12; 1 Timothy 5:17–18; 1 Corinthians 9:7–15
7 Joel 2:12–13; 1 Corinthians 7:5
8 Deuteronomy 6:13
9 Psalm 76:11
10 Acts 17:16–17; Psalm 16:4
11 Deuteronomy 7:5; Isaiah 30:22
12 Numbers 15:39
13 Deuteronomy 13:6–8
14 Hosea 5:11; Micah 6:16
15 1 Kings 11:33; 1 Kings 12:33
16 Deuteronomy 12:30–32
17 Deuteronomy 4:15–19; Acts 17:29; Romans 1:21–23, 25
18 Daniel 3:18; Galatians 4:8
19 Exodus 32:5
20 Exodus 32:8
21 1 Kings 18:26, 28; Isaiah 65:11
22 Acts 17:22; Colossians 2:21–23
23 Malachi 1:7–8, 14
24 Deuteronomy 4:2

invented and taken up of ourselves,[1] or received by tradition from others,[2] though under the title of antiquity,[3] custom,[4] devotion,[5] good intent, or any other pretence whatsoever;[6] simony [selling something spiritual]; [7] sacrilege; [8] all neglect,[9] contempt,[10] hindering,[11] and opposing the worship and ordinances which God has appointed.[12]

Q. 110. *What are the reasons annexed to the second commandment, the more to enforce it?*

A. The reasons annexed to the second commandment, the more to enforce it, contained in these words, For I the Lord your God am a jealous God, visiting the iniquity of the fathers on the children to the third and fourth generation of those who hate me; and showing steadfast love to thousands of those who love me, and keep my commandments;[13] are, besides God's sovereignty over us, and propriety in us,[14] his fervent zeal for his own worship,[15] and his revengeful indignation against all false worship, as being a spiritual whoredom;[16] accounting the breakers of this commandment such as hate him, and threatening to punish them unto divers [various] generations;[17] and esteeming the observers of it such as love him and keep his commandments, and promising mercy to them unto many generations.[18]

Q. 111. *Which is the third commandment?*

A. The third commandment is, You shall not take the name of the Lord

---

1   Psalm 106:39
2   Matthew 15:9
3   1 Peter 1:18
4   Jeremiah 44:17
5   Isaiah 65:3–5; Galatians 1:13–14
6   1 Samuel 13:11–12; 15:21
7   Acts 8:18
8   Romans 2:22; Malachi 3:8
9   Exodus 4:24–26
10 Matthew 22:5; Malachi 1:7, 13
11 Matthew 23:13
12 Acts 13:44–45; 1 Thessalonians 2:15–16
13 Exodus 20:5–6
14 Psalm 45:11; Revelation 15:3–4
15 Exodus 34:13–14
16 1 Corinthians 10:20–22; Deuteronomy 32:16–20
17 Hosea 2:2–4
18 Deuteronomy 5:29

your God in vain, for the Lord will not hold him guiltless who takes his name in vain.[1]

Q. 112. *What is required in the third commandment?*

A The third commandment requires, that the name of God, his titles, attributes,[2] ordinances,[3] the Word,[4] sacraments,[5] prayer,[6] oaths,[7] vows,[8] lots,[9] his work,[10] and whatsoever else there is whereby he makes himself known, be holily and reverently used in thought,[11] meditation,[12] word,[13] and writing;[14] by a holy profession,[15] and answerable conversation,[16] to the glory of God,[17] and the good of ourselves,[18] and others.[19]

Q. 113. *What are the sins forbidden in the third commandment?*

A. The sins forbidden in the third commandment are, the not using of God's name as is required;[20] and the abuse of it in an ignorant,[21] vain,[22] irreverent, profane,[23] superstitious[24] or wicked mentioning or otherwise using his titles, attributes,[25] ordinances,[26] or works,[27]

---

1   Exodus 20:7
2   Matthew 11:9; Deuteronomy 28:58; Psalm 29:2; 68:4; Revelation 15:3–4
3   Malachi 1:14; Ecclesiastes 5:1
4   Psalm 138:2
5   1 Corinthians 11:24–25, 28–29
6   1 Timothy 2:8
7   Jeremiah 4:2
8   Ecclesiastes 5:2, 4–6
9   Acts 1:24, 26
10 Job 36:24
11 Malachi 3:16
12 Psalm 8:1, 3–4, 9
13 Colossians 3:17; Psalm 105:2, 5
14 Psalm 102:18
15 1 Peter 3:15; Micah 4:5
16 Philippians 1:27
17 1 Corinthians 10:31
18 Jeremiah 32:39
19 1 Peter 2:12
20 Malachi 2:2
21 Acts 17:23
22 Proverbs 30:9
23 Malachi 1:6–7, 12; 3:14
24 1 Samuel 4:3–5; Jeremiah 7:4, 9–10, 14, 31; Colossians 2:20–22
25 2 Kings 18:30, 35; Exodus 5:2; Psalm 139:20
26 Psalm 50:16–17
27 Isaiah 5:12

by blasphemy,[1] perjury;[2] all sinful cursings,[3] oaths,[4] vows,[5] and lots;[6] violating of our oaths and vows, if lawful;[7] and fulfilling them, if of things unlawful;[8] murmuring and quarrelling at,[9] curious prying into,[10] and misapplying of God's decrees[11] and providences;[12] misinterpreting,[13] misapplying,[14] or any way perverting the Word, or any part of it;[15] to profane jests,[16] curious or unprofitable questions, vain janglings [discussion], or the maintaining of false doctrines;[17] abusing it, the creatures, or anything contained under the name of God, to charms [witchcraft],[18] or sinful lusts and practices;[19] the maligning,[20] scorning,[21] reviling,[22] or in any way opposing God's truth, grace, and ways;[23] making profession of religion in hypocrisy or for sinister ends;[24] being ashamed of it,[25] or a shame to it, by unconformable,[26] unwise,[27] unfruitful,[28] and offensive walking,[29] or backsliding from it.[30]

---

1   2 Kings 19:22; Leviticus 24:11
2   Zechariah 5:4; 8:17
3   1 Samuel 17:43; 2 Samuel 16:5
4   Jeremiah 5:7; 23:10
5   Deuteronomy 23:18; Acts 23:12, 14
6   Esther 3:7; 9:24; Psalm 22:18
7   Psalm 24:4; Ezekiel 17:16, 18–19
8   Mark 6:26; 1 Samuel 25:22, 32–34
9   Romans 9:14, 19–20
10 Deuteronomy 29:29
11 Romans 3:5, 7; 6:1
12 Ecclesiastes 8:11; 9:3; Psalm 39
13 Matthew 5:21–22
14 Ezekiel 13:22
15 2 Peter 3:16; Matthew 22:24–31; 25:28–30
16 Isaiah 22:13; Jeremiah 23:34, 36, 38
17 1 Timothy 1:4, 6–7; 6:4–5, 20; 2 Timothy 2:14; Titus 3:9
18 Deuteronomy 18:10–14; Acts 19:13
19 2 Timothy 4:3–4; Romans 13:13–14; 1 Kings 21:9–10; Jude 4
20 Acts 13:45; 1 John 3:12
21 Psalm 1:1; 2 Peter 3:3
22 1 Peter 4:4
23 Acts 13:45–46, 50; Acts 4:18; Acts 19:9; 1 Thessalonians 2:16; Hebrews 10:29
24 2 Timothy 3:5; Matthew 23:14; 6:1–2, 5, 16
25 Mark 8:38
26 Psalm 73:14–15
27 1 Corinthians 6:5–6; Ephesians 5:15–17
28 Isaiah 5:4; 2 Peter 1:8–9
29 Romans 2:23–24
30 Galatians 3:1, 3; Hebrews 6:6

Q. 114. *What reasons are annexed to the third commandment?*

A. The reasons annexed to the third commandment, in these words, The Lord your God, and, For the Lord will not hold him guiltless who takes his name in vain,[1] are, because he is the Lord and our God, therefore his name is not to be profaned, or any way abused by us;[2] especially because he will be so far from acquitting and sparing the transgressors of this commandment, as that he will not suffer them to escape his righteous judgment;[3] albeit many such escape the censures and punishments of men.[4]

Q. 115. *Which is the fourth commandment?*

A. The fourth commandment is, Remember the Sabbath day, to keep it holy. Six days you shall labour, and do all your work; but the seventh day is a Sabbath to the Lord your God: on it you shall not do any work, you, nor your son, nor your daughter, your male-servant, nor your female servant, nor your cattle, nor the sojourner who is within your gates. For in six days the Lord made heaven and earth, the sea, and all that in them is, and rested on the seventh day. Therefore the Lord blessed the Sabbath-day and made it holy.[5]

Q. 116. *What is required in the fourth commandment?*

A. The fourth commandment requires of all men the sanctifying or keeping holy to God such set times as he has appointed in his Word, expressly one whole day in seven; which was the seventh from the beginning of the world to the resurrection of Christ, and the first day of the week ever since, and so to continue to the end of the world; which is the Christian Sabbath,[6] and in the New Testament called The Lord's Day.[7]

Q. 117. *How is the Sabbath or the Lord's Day to be sanctified?*

A. The Sabbath or Lord's Day is to be sanctified by a holy resting all the day,[8] not only from such works as are at all times sinful, but even from such worldly employments and recreations as are on other

---

1   Exodus 20:7
2   Leviticus 19:12
3   Ezekiel 36:21–23; Deuteronomy 28:58–59; Zechariah 5:2–4
4   1 Samuel 2:12, 17, 22, 24 compared with 1 Samuel 3:13
5   Exodus 20:8–11
6   Deuteronomy 5:12–14; Genesis 2:2–3; 1 Corinthians 16:1–2; Matthew 5:17–18; Isaiah 56:2, 4, 6–7
7   Revelation 1:10
8   Exodus 20:8, 10

days lawful;[1] and making it our delight to spend the whole time (except so much of it as is to be taken up in works of necessity and mercy)[2] in the public and private exercises of God's worship:[3] and, to that end, we are to prepare our hearts, and with such foresight, diligence, and moderation, to dispose and seasonably dispatch our worldly business, that we may be the more free and fit for the duties of that day.[4]

Q. 118. *Why is the charge of keeping the Sabbath more specially directed to governors of families, and other superiors?*

A. The charge of keeping the Sabbath is more specially directed to governors of families, and other superiors, because they are bound not only to keep it themselves, but to see that it be observed by all those that are under their charge; and because they are prone often to hinder them by employments of their own.[5]

Q. 119. *What are the sins forbidden in the fourth commandment?*

A. The sins forbidden in the fourth commandment are, all omissions of the duties required,[6] all careless, negligent, and unprofitable performing of them, and being weary of them;[7] all profaning the day by idleness, and doing that which is in itself sinful;[8] and by all needless works, words, and thoughts, about our worldly employments and recreations.[9]

Q. 120. *What are the reasons annexed to the fourth commandment, the more to enforce it?*

A. The reasons annexed to the fourth commandment, the more to enforce it, are taken from the equity of it, God allowing us six days of seven for our own affairs, and reserving but one for himself in these words, Six days you shall labour, and do all your work:[10] from God's challenging a special propriety in that day, The seventh day is the Sabbath of the Lord your God:[11] from the example of God, who

---

1   Exodus 16:25–28; Nehemiah 13:15–22; Jeremiah 17:21–22
2   Matthew 12:1–13
3   Isaiah 58:13; Luke 4:16; Acts 20:7; 1 Corinthians 16:1–2; Psalm 92 [title]; Isaiah 66:23; Leviticus 23:3
4   Exodus 20:8; Luke 23:54, 56; Exodus 16:22, 25–26, 29; Nehemiah 13:19
5   Exodus 20:10; Joshua 24:15; Nehemiah 13:15, 17; Jeremiah 17:20–22; Exodus 23:12
6   Ezekiel 22:26
7   Acts 20:7, 9; Ezekiel 33:30–32; Amos 8:5; Malachi 1:13
8   Ezekiel 23:38
9   Jeremiah 17:24, 27; Isaiah 58:13
10   Exodus 20:9
11   Exodus 20:10

in six days made heaven and earth, the sea, and all that in them is, and rested the seventh day: and from that blessing which God put upon that day, not only in sanctifying it to be a day for his service, but in ordaining it to be a means of blessing to us in our sanctifying it; Therefore the Lord blessed the Sabbath day, and made it holy.[1]

Q. 121. *Why is the word Remember set in the beginning of the fourth commandment?*

A. The word Remember is set in the beginning of the fourth commandment,[2] partly, because of the great benefit of remembering it, we being thereby helped in our preparation to keep it,[3] and, in keeping it, better to keep all the rest of the commandments,[4] and to continue a thankful remembrance of the two great benefits of creation and redemption, which contain a short abridgment of religion;[5] and partly, because we are very ready to forget it,[6] for that there is less light of nature for it,[7] and yet it restrains our natural liberty in things at other times lawful;[8] that it comes but once in seven days, and many worldly businesses come between, and too often take off our minds from thinking of it, either to prepare for it, or to sanctify it;[9] and that Satan with his instruments labours much to blot out the glory, and even the memory of it, to bring in all irreligion and impiety.[10]

Q. 122. *What is the sum of the six commandments which contain our duty to man?*

A. The sum of the six commandments which contain our duty to man, is, to love our neighbour as ourselves,[11] and to do to others what we would have them to do to us.[12]

Q. 123. *Which is the fifth commandment?*

A. The fifth commandment is, Honour your father and your mother:

---

1   Exodus 20:11
2   Exodus 20:8
3   Exodus 16:23; Luke 23:54–56 compared with Mark 15:42; Nehemiah 13:19
4   Psalm 92 [title] compared with verses 13–14; Ezekiel 20:12, 19–20
5   Genesis 2:2–3; Psalm 118:22, 24 compared with Acts 4:10–11; Revelation 1:10
6   Ezekiel 22:26
7   Nehemiah 9:14
8   Exodus 34:21
9   Deuteronomy 5:14–15; Amos 8:5
10   Lamentations 1:7; Jeremiah 17:21–23; Nehemiah 13:15–23
11   Matthew 22:39
12   Matthew 7:12

that your days may be long in the land which the Lord your God is giving you.[1]

Q. 124. *Who are meant by father and mother in the fifth commandment?*

A. By father and mother, in the fifth commandment, are meant, not only natural parents,[2] but all superiors in age[3] and gifts;[4] and especially such as, by God's ordinance, are over us in place of authority, whether in family,[5] church,[6] or commonwealth.[7]

Q. 125. *Why are superiors styled father and mother?*

A. Superiors are styled father and mother, both to teach them in all duties toward their inferiors, like natural parents, to express love and tenderness to them, according to their several relations;[8] and to work inferiors to a greater willingness and cheerfulness in performing their duties to their superiors, as to their parents.[9]

Q. 126. *What is the general scope of the fifth commandment?*

A. The general scope of the fifth commandment is, the performance of those duties which we mutually owe in our several relations, as inferiors [those under authority], superiors [those in authority], or equals.[10]

Q. 127. *What is the honour that inferiors owe to their superiors?*

A. The honour which inferiors owe to their superiors is, all due reverence in heart,[11] word,[12] and behaviour;[13] prayer and thanksgiving for them;[14] imitation of their virtues and graces;[15] willing obedience to their lawful commands and counsels;[16]

---

1 Exodus 20:12
2 Proverbs 23:22, 25; Ephesians 6:1–2
3 1 Timothy 5:1–2
4 Genesis 4:20–22; 45:8
5 2 Kings 5:13
6 2 Kings 2:12; 13:14; Galatians 4:19
7 Isaiah 49:23
8 Ephesians 6:4; 2 Corinthians 12:14; 1 Thessalonians 2:7–8, 11; Numbers 11:11–12
9 1 Corinthians 4:14–16; 2 Kings 5:13
10 Ephesians 5:21; 1 Peter 2:17; Romans 12:10
11 Malachi 1:6; Leviticus 19:3
12 Proverbs 31:28; 1 Peter 3:6
13 Leviticus 19:32; 1 Kings 2:19
14 1 Timothy 2:1–2
15 Hebrews 13:7; Philippians 3:17
16 Ephesians 6:1–2, 6–7; 1 Peter 2:13–14; Romans 13:1–5; Hebrews 13:17; Proverbs 4:3–4; 23:22; Exodus 18:19, 24

due submission to their corrections;[1] fidelity to,[2] defence,[3] and maintenance of their persons and authority, according to their several ranks, and the nature of their places;[4] bearing with their infirmities, and covering them in love,[5] that so they may be an honour to them and to their government.[6]

Q. 128. *What are the sins of inferiors against their superiors?*

A. The sins of inferiors against their superiors are, all neglect of the duties required toward them;[7] envying at,[8] contempt of,[9] and rebellion[10] against, their persons[11] and places,[12] in their lawful counsels,[13] commands, and corrections;[14] cursing, mocking[15] and all such refractory and scandalous carriage, as proves a shame and dishonour to them and their government.[16]

Q. 129. *What is required of superiors towards their inferiors?*

A. It is required of superiors, according to that power they receive from God, and that relation wherein they stand, to love,[17] pray for,[18] and bless their inferiors;[19] to instruct,[20] counsel, and admonish them;[21] countenancing,[22] commending,[23] and rewarding such as do well;[24] and discountenancing,[25] reproving, and chastising such as do ill;[26]

---

1   Hebrews 12:9; 1 Peter 2:18–20
2   Titus 2:9–10
3   1 Samuel 26:15–16; 2 Samuel 18:3; Esther 6:2
4   Matthew 22:21; Romans 13:6–7; 1 Timothy 5:17–18; Galatians 6:6; Genesis 45:11; Genesis 47:12
5   1 Peter 2:18; Proverbs 23:22; Genesis 9:23
6   Psalm 127:3–5; Proverbs 31:23
7   Matthew 15:4–6
8   Numbers 11:28–29
9   1 Samuel 8:7; Isaiah 3:5
10 2 Samuel 15:1–12
11 Exodus 24:15
12 1 Samuel 10:27
13 1 Samuel 2:25
14 Deuteronomy 21:18–21
15 Proverbs 30:11, 17
16 Proverbs 19:26
17 Colossians 3:19; Titus 2:4
18 1 Samuel 12:23; Job 1:5
19 1 Kings 8:55–56; Hebrews 7:7; Genesis 49:28
20 Deuteronomy 6:6–7
21 Ephesians 6:4
22 1 Peter 3:7
23 1 Peter 2:14; Romans 13:3
24 Esther 6:3
25 Romans 13:3–4
26 Proverbs 29:15; 1 Peter 2:14

protecting,[1] and providing for them all things necessary for soul[2] and body:[3] and by grave, wise, holy, and exemplary carriage, to procure [obtain] glory to God,[4] honour to themselves,[5] and so to preserve that authority which God has put upon them.[6]

Q. 130. *What are the sins of superiors?*

A. The sins of superiors are, besides the neglect of the duties required of them,[7] and inordinate seeking of themselves,[8] their own glory,[9] ease, profit, or pleasure;[10] commanding things unlawful,[11] or not in the power of inferiors to perform;[12] counselling,[13] encouraging,[14] or favouring them in that which is evil;[15] dissuading, discouraging, or discountenancing them in that which is good;[16] correcting them unduly;[17] careless exposing, or leaving them to wrong, temptation, and danger;[18] provoking them to wrath;[19] or any way dishonouring themselves, or lessening their authority, by an unjust, indiscreet, rigorous, or remiss behaviour.[20]

Q. 131. *What are the duties of equals?*

A. The duties of equals are, to regard the dignity and worth of each other,[21] in giving honour to go one before another;[22] and to rejoice in each others' gifts and advancement, as their own.[23]

---

1   Job 29:12–17; Isaiah 1:10–17
2   Ephesians 6:4
3   1 Timothy 5:8
4   1 Timothy 4:12; Titus 2:3–5
5   1 Kings 3:28
6   Titus2:15
7   Ezekiel 34:2–4
8   Philippians 2:21
9   John 5:44; 7:18
10   Isaiah 56:10–11; Deuteronomy 17:17
11   Daniel 3:4–6; Acts 4:17–18
12   Exodus 5:10–18; Matthew 23:2, 4
13   Matthew 14:8 compared with Mark 6:24
14   2 Samuel 13:28
15   1 Samuel 3:13
16   John 7:46–49; Colossians 3:21; Exodus 5:17
17   1 Peter 2:18–20; Hebrews 12:10; Deuteronomy 25:3
18   Genesis 38:11, 26; Acts 18:17
19   Ephesians 6:4
20   Genesis 9:21; 1 Kings 12:13–16; 1:6; 1 Samuel 2:29–31
21   1 Peter 2:17
22   Romans 12:10
23   Romans 12:15–16; Philippians 2:3–4

Q. 132. *What are the sins of equals?*
A. The sins of equals are, besides the neglect of the duties required,[1] the undervaluing of the worth,[2] envying the gifts,[3] grieving at the advancement of prosperity one of another;[4] and usurping pre-eminence one over another.[5]

Q. 133. *What is the reason annexed to the fifth commandment, the more to enforce it?*
A. The reason annexed to the fifth commandment, in these words, That your days may be long in the land which the Lord your God is giving you,[6] is an express promise of long life and prosperity, as far as it shall serve for God's glory and their own good, to all such as keep this commandment.[7]

Q. 134. *Which is the sixth commandment?*
A. The sixth commandment is, You shall not kill.[8]

Q. 135. *What are the duties required in the sixth commandment?*
A. The duties required in the sixth commandment are all careful studies, and lawful endeavours, to preserve the life of ourselves[9] and others[10] by resisting all thoughts and purposes,[11] subduing all passions,[12] and avoiding all occasions,[13] temptations,[14] and practices, which tend to the unjust taking away the life of any;[15] by just defence thereof against violence,[16] patient bearing of the hand of God,[17] quietness of mind,[18] cheerfulness of spirit;[19] a sober use of meat,[20]

1 Romans 13:8
2 2 Timothy 3:3
3 Acts 7:9; Galatians 5:26
4 Numbers 12:2; Esther 6:12–13
5 3 John 9; Luke 22:24
6 Exodus 20:12
7 Deuteronomy 5:16; 1 Kings 8:25; Ephesians 6:2–3
8 Exodus 20:13
9 Ephesians 5:28–29
10 1 Kings 18:4
11 Jeremiah 26:15-16; Acts 23:12, 16–17, 21, 27
12 Ephesians 4:26–27
13 2 Samuel 2:22; Deuteronomy 22:8
14 Matthew 4:6-7; Proverbs 1:10–11, 15–16
15 1 Samuel 24:12; 26:9–11; Genesis 37:21–22
16 Psalm 82:4; Proverbs 24:11–12
17 James 5:7–11; Hebrews 12:9
18 1 Thessalonians 4:11; 1 Peter 3:3–4; Psalm 37:8–11
19 Proverbs 17:22
20 Proverbs 25:16, 27

drink,[1] physic [medicine],[2] sleep,[3] labour,[4] and recreations;[5] by charitable thoughts,[6] love,[7] compassion,[8] meekness, gentleness, kindness;[9] peaceable,[10] mild and courteous speeches and behaviour;[11] forbearance, readiness to be reconciled, patient bearing and forgiving of injuries, and requiting good for evil;[12] comforting and succouring the distressed and protecting and defending the innocent.[13]

Q. 136. *What are the sins forbidden in the sixth commandment?*

A. The sins forbidden in the sixth commandment are, all taking away the life of ourselves,[14] or of others,[15] except in case of public justice,[16] lawful war,[17] or necessary defence;[18] the neglecting or withdrawing the lawful and necessary means of preservation of life;[19] sinful anger,[20] hatred,[21] envy,[22] desire of revenge;[23] all excessive passions,[24] distracting cares;[25] immoderate use of meat, drink,[26] labour,[27] and recreations;[28] provoking words,[29] oppression,[30] quarrelling,[31]

1   1 Timothy 5:23
2   Isaiah 38:21
3   Psalm 127:2
4   Ecclesiastes 5:12; 2 Thessalonians 3:10, 12; Proverbs 16:26
5   Ecclesiastes 3:4, 11
6   1 Samuel 19:4–5; 22:13–14
7   Romans 13:10
8   Luke 10:33–34
9   Colossians 3:12–13
10   James 3:17
11   1 Peter 3:8–11; Proverbs 15:1; Judges 8:1–3
12   Matthew 5:24; Ephesians 5:2, 32; Romans 12:17, 20–21
13   1 Thessalonians 5:14; Job 31:19–20; Matthew 25:35–36; Proverbs 31:8–9
14   Acts 16:28
15   Genesis 9:6
16   Numbers 35:31, 33
17   Jeremiah 48:10; Deuteronomy 20
18   Exodus 22:2–3
19   Matthew 25:42–43; James 2:15–16; Ecclesiastes 6:1–2
20   Matthew 5:22
21   1 John 3:15; Leviticus 19:17
22   Proverbs 14:30
23   Romans 12:19
24   Ephesians 4:31
25   Matthew 6:31, 34
26   Luke 21:34; Romans 13:13
27   Ecclesiastes 12:12; 2:22–23
28   Isaiah 5:12
29   Proverbs 15:1; 12:18
30   Ezekiel 18:18; Exodus 1:14
31   Galatians 5:15; Proverbs 23:29

striking, wounding,[1] and whatsoever else tends to the destruction of the life of any.[2]

Q. 137. *Which is the seventh commandment?*

A. The seventh commandment is, You shall not commit adultery.[3]

Q. 138. *What are the duties required in the seventh commandment?*

A. The duties required in the seventh commandment are, chastity in body, mind, affections,[4] words,[5] and behaviour;[6] and the preservation of it in ourselves and others;[7] watchfulness over the eyes and all the senses;[8] temperance,[9] keeping of chaste company,[10] modesty in apparel;[11] marriage by those that have not the gift of continence,[12] conjugal love,[13] and cohabitation;[14] diligent labour in our callings;[15] shunning all occasions of uncleanness, and resisting temptations thereunto.[16]

Q. 139. *What are the sins forbidden in the seventh commandment?*

A. The sins forbidden in the seventh commandment, besides the neglect of the duties required,[17] are, adultery, fornication,[18] rape, incest,[19] sodomy, and all unnatural lusts;[20] all unclean imaginations, thoughts, purposes, and affections;[21] all corrupt or filthy communications, or listening thereunto;[22] wanton looks,[23]

---

1   Numbers 35:16–18, 21
2   Exodus 21:18–36
3   Exodus 20:14
4   1 Thessalonians 4:4; Job 31:1; 1 Corinthians 7:34
5   Colossians 4:6
6   1 Peter 2:3
7   1 Corinthians 7:2, 35–36
8   Job 31:1
9   Acts 24:24–25
10 Proverbs 2:16–20
11 1 Timothy 2:9
12 1 Corinthians 7:2, 9
13 Proverbs 5:19–20
14 1 Peter 3:7
15 Proverbs 31:11, 27–28
16 Proverbs 5:8; Genesis 39:8–10
17 Proverbs 5:7
18 Hebrews 13:4; Galatians 5:19
19 2 Samuel 13:14; 1 Corinthians 5:1
20 Romans 1:24, 26–27; Leviticus 20:15–16
21 Matthew 5:28; 15:19; Colossians 3:5
22 Ephesians 5:3–4; Proverbs 7:5, 21–22
23 Isaiah 3:16; 2 Peter 2:14

impudent or light behaviour, immodest apparel;[1] prohibiting of lawful,[2] and dispensing with unlawful marriages;[3] allowing, tolerating, keeping of stews [brothels], and resorting to them;[4] entangling vows of single life,[5] undue delay of marriage,[6] having more wives or husbands than one at the same time;[7] unjust divorce,[8] or desertion;[9] idleness, gluttony, drunkenness,[10] unchaste company;[11] lascivious songs, books, pictures, dancing, stage plays;[12] and all other provocations to, or acts of uncleanness, either in ourselves or others.[13]

Q. 140. *Which is the eighth commandment?*
A. The eighth commandment is, You shall not steal.[14]

Q. 141. *What are the duties required in the eighth commandment?*
A. The duties required in the eighth commandment are, truth, faithfulness, and justice in contracts and commerce between man and man;[15] rendering to everyone his due;[16] restitution of goods unlawfully detained from the right owners thereof;[17] giving and lending freely, according to our abilities, and the necessities of others;[18] moderation of our judgments, wills, and affections concerning worldly goods;[19] a provident care and study to get,[20] keep, use, and dispose these things which are necessary and convenient for the sustentation of our nature, and suitable to our

---

1   Proverbs 7:10, 13
2   1 Timothy 4:3
3   Leviticus 18:1–21; Mark 6:18; Malachi 2:11–12
4   1 Kings 15:12; 2 Kings 23:7; Deuteronomy 23:17–18; Leviticus 19:29; Jeremiah 5:7; Proverbs 7:24–27
5   Matthew 19:10–11
6   1 Corinthians 7:7–9; Genesis 38:26
7   Malachi 2:14–15; Matthew 19:5
8   Malachi 2:16; Matthew 5:32
9   1 Corinthians 7:12–13
10 Ezekiel 16:49; Proverbs 23:30–33
11 Genesis 39:10; Proverbs 5:8
12 Ephesians 5:4; Ezekiel 23:14–16; Isaiah 23:15–17; 3:16; Mark 6:22; Romans 13:13; 1 Peter 4:3
13 2 Kings 9:30 compared with Jeremiah 4:30 and with Ezekiel 23:40
14 Exodus 20:15
15 Psalm 15:2, 4; Zechariah 7:4, 10; 8:16–17
16 Romans 13:7
17 Leviticus 6:2–5 compared with Luke 19:8
18 Luke 6:30, 38; 1 John 3:17; Ephesians 4:28; Galatians 6:10
19 1 Timothy 6:6–9; Galatians 6:14
20 1 Timothy 5:8

condition;[1] a lawful calling,[2] and diligence in it;[3] frugality;[4] avoiding unnecessary lawsuits,[5] and suretyship, or other like engagements;[6] and an endeavour, by all just and lawful means, to procure [obtain], preserve, and further the wealth and outward estate of others, as well as our own.[7]

Q. 142. *What are the sins forbidden in the eighth commandment?*

A. The sins forbidden in the eighth commandment, besides the neglect of the duties required,[8] are, theft,[9] robbery,[10] man-stealing [kidnapping],[11] and receiving any thing that is stolen;[12] fraudulent dealing,[13] false weights and measures,[14] removing landmarks,[15] injustice and unfaithfulness incontracts between man and man,[16] or in matters of trust;[17] oppression,[18] extortion,[19] usury [unreasonable interest],[20] bribery,[21] vexatious lawsuits,[22] unjust enclosures and depopulations;[23] engrossing commodities to enhance the price;[24] unlawful callings,[25] and all other unjust or sinful ways of taking or withholding from our neighbour what belongs to him, orof enriching ourselves;[26] covetousness;[27] inordinate prizing and

---

1   Proverbs 27:23-27; Ecclesiastes 2:2; 3:12-13; 1 Timothy 6:17-18; Isaiah 38:1; Matthew 11:8
2   1 Corinthians 7:20; Genesis 2:15; 3:19
3   Ephesians 4:28; Proverbs 10:4
4   John 6:12; Proverbs 21:20
5   1 Corinthians 6:1-9
6   Proverbs 6:1-6; 11:15
7   Leviticus 25:35; Deuteronomy 22:1-4; Exodus 23:4-5; Genesis 47:14, 20; Philippians 2:4; Matthew 22:39
8   James 2:15-16; 1 John 3:17
9   Ephesians 4:28
10   Psalm 62:10
11   1 Timothy 1:10
12   Proverbs 29:24; Psalm 50:18
13   1 Thessalonians 4:6
14   Proverbs 11:1; 20:10
15   Deuteronomy 19:14; Proverbs 23:10
16   Amos 8:5; Psalm 37:21
17   Luke 16:10-12
18   Ezekiel 22:29; Leviticus 25:17
19   Matthew 23:25; Ezekiel 22:12
20   Psalm 15:5
21   Job 15:34
22   1 Corinthians 6:6-8; Proverbs 3:29-30
23   Isaiah 5:8; Micah 2:2
24   Proverbs 11:26
25   Acts 19:19, 24-25
26   Job 20:19; James 5:4; Proverbs 21:6
27   Luke 12:15

affecting worldly goods;[1] distrustful and distracting cares and studies in getting, keeping, and using them;[2] envying at the prosperity of others;[3] as likewise idleness,[4] prodigality, wasteful gaming; and all other ways whereby we do unduly prejudice our own outward estate,[5] and defrauding ourselves of the due use and comfort of that estate which God has given us.[6]

Q. 143. *Which is the ninth commandment?*

A. The ninth commandment is, You shall not bear false witness against your neighbour.[7]

Q. 144. *What are the duties required in the ninth commandment?*

A. The duties required in the ninth commandment are, the preserving and promoting of truth between man and man,[8] and the good name of our neighbour, as well as our own;[9] appearing and standing for the truth;[10] and from the heart,[11] sincerely,[12] freely,[13] clearly,[14] and fully,[15] speaking the truth, and only the truth, in matters of judgment and justice,[16] and in all other things whatsoever;[17] a charitable esteem of our neighbours;[18] loving, desiring, and rejoicing in their good name;[19] sorrowing for,[20] and covering of their infirmities;[21] freely acknowledging of their gifts and graces,[22]

---

1   1 Timothy 6:5; Colossians 3:2; Proverbs 23:5; Psalm 62:10
2   Matthew 6:25, 31, 34; Ecclesiastes 5:12
3   Psalm 73:3; 37:1, 7
4   2 Thessalonians 3:11; Proverbs 18:9
5   Proverbs 21:7; 23:20–21; 28:19
6   Ecclesiastes 4:8; 6:2; 1 Timothy 5:8
7   Exodus 20:16
8   Zechariah 8:16
9   3 John 12
10   Proverbs 31:8–9
11   Psalm 15:2
12   2 Chronicles 19:9
13   1 Samuel 19:4–5
14   Joshua 7:19
15   2 Samuel 14:18–20
16   Leviticus 19:15; Proverbs 14:5, 25
17   2 Corinthians 1:17–18; Ephesians 4:25
18   Hebrews 6:9; 1 Corinthians 13:7
19   Romans 1:8; 2 John 4; 3 John 3–4
20   2 Corinthians 2:4; 12:21
21   Proverbs 17:9; 1 Peter 4:8
22   1 Corinthians 1:4–5, 7; 2 Timothy 1:4–5

defending their innocence;[1] a ready receiving of a good report,[2] and unwillingness to admit of an evil report,[3] concerning them; discouraging tale-bearers,[4] flatterers,[5] and slanderers;[6] love and care of our own good name, and defending it when need requires;[7] keeping of lawful promises;[8] studying and practicing of whatsoever things are true, honest, lovely, and of good report.[9]

Q. 145. *What are the sins forbidden in the ninth commandment?*

A. The sins forbidden in the ninth commandment are, all prejudicing the truth, and the good name of our neighbours, as well as our own,[10] especially in public judicature;[11] giving false evidence,[12] suborning [bribing] false witnesses,[13] wittingly appearing and pleading for an evil cause, outfacing and overbearing the truth;[14] passing unjust sentence,[15] calling evil good, and good evil; rewarding the wicked according to the work of the righteous, and the righteous according to the work of the wicked;[16] forgery,[17] concealing the truth, undue silence in a just cause,[18] and holding our peace when iniquity calls for either a reproof from ourselves,[19] or complaint to others;[20] speaking the truth unseasonably,[21] or maliciously to a wrong end,[22] or perverting it to a wrong meaning,[23] or in doubtful and equivocal expressions, to the prejudice of truth or justice;[24]

---

1 1 Samuel 22:14
2 1 Corinthians 13:6–7
3 Psalm 15:3
4 Proverbs 25:23
5 Proverbs 26:24–25
6 Psalm 101:5
7 Proverbs 22:1; John 8:49
8 Psalm 15:4
9 Philippians 4:8
10 1 Samuel 17:28; 2 Samuel 16:3; 1:9–10, 15–16
11 Leviticus 19:19; Habakkuk 1:4
12 Proverbs 19:5; Proverbs 6:16, 19
13 Acts 6:13
14 Jeremiah 9:3, 5; Acts 24:2, 5; Psalm 12:3–4; Psalm 52:1–4
15 Proverbs 17:15; 1 Kings 21:9–14
16 Isaiah 5:23
17 Psalm 119:69; Luke 19:8; 16:5–7
18 Leviticus 5:1; Deuteronomy 13:8; Acts 5:3, 8–9; 2 Timothy 4:6
19 1 Kings 1:6; Leviticus 19:17
20 Isaiah 59:4
21 Proverbs 29:11
22 1 Samuel 22:9–10 compared with Psalm 52 [title], verses 1–5
23 Psalm 56:5; John 2:19 compared with Matthew 26:60–61
24 Genesis 3:5, 26:7, 9

speaking untruth,[1] lying ,[2] slandering,[3] backbiting,[4] detracting,[5] tale bearing,[6] whispering,[7] scoffing,[8] reviling,[9] rash,[10] harsh,[11] and partial censuring;[12] misconstruing intentions, words, and actions;[13] flattering,[14] vain-glorious boasting;[15] thinking or speaking too highly or too meanly of ourselves or others;[16] denying the gifts and graces of God;[17] aggravating smaller faults;[18] hiding, excusing, or extenuating of sins, when called to a free confession;[19] unnecessary discovering of infirmities;[20] raising false rumours,[21] receiving and countenancing evil reports,[22] and stopping our ears against just defence;[23] evil suspicion;[24] envying or grieving at the deserved credit of any,[25] endeavouring or desiring to impair it,[26] rejoicing in their disgrace and infamy;[27] scornful contempt,[28] fond admiration;[29] breach of lawful promises;[30] neglecting such things as are of good report,[31]

---

1   Isaiah 59:13
2   Leviticus 19:11; Colossians 3:9
3   Psalm 50:20
4   Psalm 15:3
5   James 4:11; Jeremiah 38:4
6   Leviticus 19:16
7   Romans 1:29–30
8   Genesis 21:9 compared with Galatians 4:29
9   1 Corinthians 6:10
10   Matthew 7:1
11   Acts 28:4
12   Genesis 38:24; Romans 2:1
13   Nehemiah 6:6–8; Romans 3:8; Psalm 69:10; 1 Samuel 1:13–15; 2 Samuel 10:3
14   Psalm 12:2–3
15   2 Timothy 3:2
16   Luke 18:9, 11; Romans 12:16; 1 Corinthians 4:6; Acts 12:22; Exodus 4:10–14
17   Job 27:5–6; Job 4:6
18   Matthew 7:3–5
19   Proverbs 28:13; 30:20; Genesis 3:12–13; Jeremiah 2:35; 2 Kings 5:25; Genesis 4:9
20   Genesis 9:22; Proverbs 25:9–10
21   Exodus 23:1
22   Proverbs 29:12
23   Acts 7:56–57; Job 31:13–14
24   1 Corinthians 13:5; 1 Timothy 6:4
25   Numbers 11:29; Matthew 21:15
26   Ezra 4:12–13
27   Jeremiah 48:27
28   Psalm 35:15–16, 21; Matthew 27:28–29
29   Jude 16; Acts 12:22
30   Romans 1:31; 2 Timothy 3:3
31   1 Samuel 2:24

and practicing, or not avoiding ourselves, or not hindering what we can in others, such things as procure [obtain] an ill name.[1]

Q. 146. *Which is the tenth commandment?*

A. The tenth commandment is, You shall not covet your neighbour's house, you shall not covet your neighbour's wife, nor his male servant, nor his female servant, nor his ox, nor his donkey, nor anything that is your neighbour's.[2]

Q. 147. *What are the duties required in the tenth commandment?*

A. The duties required in the tenth commandment are, such a full contentment with our own condition,[3] and such a charitable frame of the whole soul toward our neighbour, as that all our inward motions and affections touching him, tend unto, and further all that good which is his.[4]

Q. 148. *What are the sins forbidden in the tenth commandment?*

A. The sins forbidden in the tenth commandment are discontentment with our own estate;[5] envying[6] and grieving at the good of our neighbour,[7] together with all inordinate motions and affections to anything that is his.[8]

Q. 149. *Is any man able perfectly to keep the commandments of God?*

A. No man is able, either of himself,[9] or by any grace received in this life, perfectly to keep the commandments of God;[10] but does daily break them in thought,[11] word, and deed.[12]

Q. 150. *Are all transgressions of the law of God equally heinous in themselves, and in the sight of God?*

A. All transgressions of the law of God are not equally heinous; but

---

1   2 Samuel 13:12–13; Proverbs 5:8–9; 6:33
2   Exodus 20:17
3   Hebrews 13:5; 1 Timothy 6:6
4   Job 31:29; Romans 12:15; Psalm 122:7–9; 1 Timothy 1:5; Esther 10:3; 1 Corinthians 13:4–7
5   1 Kings 21:4; Esther 5:13; 1 Corinthians 10:10
6   Galatians 5:26; James 3:14, 16
7   Psalm 112:9–10; Nehemiah 2:10
8   Romans 7:7–8; 13:9; Deuteronomy 5:21
9   James 3:2; John 15:5; Romans 8:3
10 Ecclesiastes 7:20; 1 John 1:8, 10; Galatians 5:17; Romans 7:18–19
11 Genesis 6:5; 8:21
12 Genesis 3:9–19; James 3:2–13

some sins in themselves, and by reason of several aggravations, are more heinous in the sight of God than others.[1]

Q. 151. *What are those aggravations that make some sins more heinous than others?*

A. Sins receive their aggravations,

1. From the persons offending[2] if they be of riper age,[3] greater experience or grace,[4] eminent for profession,[5] gifts,[6] place,[7] office,[8] guides to others,[9] and whose example is likely to be followed by others.[10]

2. From the parties offended:[11] if immediately against God,[12] his attributes,[13] and worship;[14] against Christ, and his grace;[15] the Holy Spirit,[16] his witness,[17] and workings [actions],[18] against superiors, men of eminency,[19] and such as we stand especially related and engaged unto;[20]against any of the saints,[21] particularly weak brethren,[22] the souls of them, or any other,[23] and the common good of all or many.[24]

3. From the nature and quality of the offense:[25] if it be against the express letter of the law,[26] break many commandments, contain

---

1   John 19:11; Ezekiel 8:6, 13, 15; 1 John 5:16; Psalm 78:17, 32, 56
2   Jeremiah 2:8
3   Job 32:7, 9; Ecclesiastes 4:13
4   1 Kings 11:4, 9
5   2 Samuel 12:14; 1 Corinthians 5:1
6   James 4:17; Luke 12:47–48
7   Jeremiah 5:4–5
8   2 Samuel 12:7–9; Ezekiel 8:11–12
9   Romans 2:17–24
10 Galatians 2:11–14
11 Matthew 21:38–39
12 1 Samuel 2:25; Acts 5:4; Psalm 5:4
13 Romans 2:4
14 Malachi 1:8, 14
15 Hebrews 2:2–3; Hebrews 12:25
16 Hebrews 10:29; Matthew 12:31–32
17 Ephesians 4:30
18 Hebrews 6:4–6
19 Jude 8; Numbers 12:8–9; Isaiah 3:5
20 Proverbs 30:17; 2 Corinthians 12:15; Psalm 55:12–15
21 Zephaniah 2:8, 10–11; Matthew 18:6; 1 Corinthians 6:8; Revelation 17:6
22 1 Corinthians 8:11–12; Romans 14:13–15, 21
23 Ezekiel 13:19; 1 Corinthians 8:12; Revelation 18:12–13; Matthew 23:15
24 1 Thessalonians 2:15–16; Joshua 22:20
25 Proverbs 6:30–35
26 Ezra 9:10–12; 1 Kings 11:9–10

in it many sins:[1] if not only conceived in the heart, but breaks forth in words and actions,[2] scandalize others,[3] and admit of no reparation:[4] if against means,[5] mercies,[6] judgments,[7] light of nature,[8] conviction of conscience,[9] public or private admonition,[10] censures of the church,[11] civil punishments;[12] and our prayers, purposes, promises,[13] vows,[14] covenants,[15] and engagements to God or men:[16] if done deliberately,[17] wilfully,[18] presumptuously,[19] impudently,[20] boastingly,[21] maliciously,[22] frequently,[23] obstinately,[24] with delight,[25] continuance,[26] or relapsing after repentance.[27]

4. From circumstances of time[28] and place:[29] if on the Lord's Day,[30] or other times of divine worship;[31] or immediately before[32] or after these,[33] or other helps to prevent or remedy such miscarriages;[34] if

---

1 Colossians 3:5; 1 Timothy 6:10; Proverbs 5:8–12; 6:32–33; Joshua 7:21
2 James 1:14–15; Matthew 5:22; Micah 2:1
3 Matthew 18:7; Romans 2:23–24
4 Deuteronomy 22:22 compared with verses 28–29; Proverbs 6:32–35
5 Matthew 11:21–24; John 15:22
6 Isaiah 1:3; Deuteronomy 32:6
7 Amos 4:8–11; Jeremiah 5:3
8 Romans 1:26–27
9 Romans 1:32; Daniel 5:22; Titus 3:10–11
10 Proverbs 29:1
11 Titus 3:10; Matthew 18:17
12 Proverbs 27:22; Proverbs 23:35
13 Psalm 78:34–37; Jeremiah 2:20; 42:5–6, 20–21
14 Ecclesiastes 5:4–6; Proverbs 20:25
15 Leviticus 26:25
16 Proverbs 2:17; Ezekiel 17:18–19
17 Psalm 36:4
18 Jeremiah 6:16
19 Numbers 15:30; Exodus 21:14
20 Jeremiah 3:3; Proverbs 7:13
21 Psalm 52:1
22 3 John 10
23 Numbers 14:22
24 Zechariah 7:11–12
25 Proverbs 2:14
26 Isaiah 57:17
27 Jeremiah 34:8–11; 2 Peter 2:20–22
28 2 Kings 5:26
29 Jeremiah 7:10; Isaiah 26:10
30 Ezekiel 23:37–29
31 Isaiah 58:3–5; Numbers 25:6–7
32 1 Corinthians 11:20–21
33 Jeremiah 7:8–10; Proverbs 7:14–15; John 13:27, 30
34 Ezra 9:13–14

in public, or in the presence of others, who are thereby likely to be provoked or defiled.[1]

Q. 152. *What does every sin deserve at the hands of God?*

A. Every sin, even the least, being against the sovereignty,[2] goodness,[3] and holiness of God,[4] and against his righteous law,[5] deserves his wrath and curse,[6] both in this life,[7] and that which is to come;[8] and cannot be expiated but by the blood of Christ.[9]

Q. 153. *What does God require of us, that we may escape his wrath and curse due to us by reason of the transgression of the law?*

A. That we may escape the wrath and curse of God due to us by reason of the transgression of the law, he requires of us repentance toward God, and faith toward our Lord Jesus Christ,[10] and the diligent use of the outward means whereby Christ communicates to us the benefits of his mediation.[11]

Q. 154. *What are the outward means whereby Christ communicates to us the benefits of his mediation?*

A. The outward and ordinary means whereby Christ communicates to his church the benefits of his mediation, are all his ordinances; especially the Word, sacraments, and prayer; all which are made effectual to the elect for their salvation.[12]

Q. 155. *How is the Word made effectual to salvation?*

A. The Spirit of God makes the reading, but especially the preaching of the Word, an effectual means of enlightening,[13] convincing, and humbling sinners;[14] of driving them out of themselves, and drawing

---

1   2 Samuel 16:22; 1 Samuel 2:22–24
2   James 2:10–11
3   Exodus 20:1–2
4   Habakkuk 1:13; Leviticus 10:3; 11:44–45
5   1 John 3:4; Romans 7:12
6   Ephesians 5:6; Galatians 3:10
7   Lamentations 3:39; Deuteronomy 28:15–68
8   Matthew 25:41
9   Hebrews 9:22; 1 Peter 1:18–19
10   Acts 20:21; Matthew 3:7–8; Luke 13:3, 5; Acts 16:30–31; John 3:16, 18
11   Proverbs 2:1–5; 8:33–36
12   Matthew 28:19–20; Acts 2:42, 46–47
13   Nehemiah 8:8; Acts 26:18; Psalm 19:8
14   1 Corinthians 14:24–25; 2 Chronicles 34:18–19, 26–28

them unto Christ;[1] of conforming them to his image,[2] and subduing them to his will;[3] of strengthening them against temptations and corruptions;[4] of building them up in grace,[5] and establishing their hearts in holiness and comfort through faith unto salvation.[6]

Q. 156. *Is the Word of God to be read by all?*
A. Although all are not to be permitted to read the Word publicly to the congregation,[7] yet all sorts of people are bound to read it apart by themselves,[8] and with their families:[9] to which end, the Holy Scriptures are to be translated out of the original into vulgar [common] languages.[10]

Q. 157. *How is the Word of God to be read?*
A. The Holy Scriptures are to be read with a high and reverent esteem of them;[11] with a firm persuasion that they are the very Word of God,[12] and that he only can enable us to understand them;[13] with desire to know, believe, and obey the will of God revealed in them;[14] with diligence,[15] and attention to the matter and scope of them;[16] with meditation,[17] application,[18] self-denial,[19] and prayer.[20]

Q. 158. *By whom is the Word of God to be preached?*
A. The Word of God is to be preached only by such as are sufficiently gifted,[21] and also duly approved and called to that office.[22]

---

1 Acts 2:37, 41; 8:27-39
2 2 Corinthians 3:18
3 2 Corinthians 10:4-6; Romans 6:17
4 Matthew 4:4, 7, 10; Ephesians 6:16-17; Psalm 19:11; 1 Corinthians 10:11
5 Acts 20:32; 2 Timothy 3:15-17
6 Romans 16:25; 1 Thessalonians 3:2, 10-11, 13; Romans 15:4; 10:13-17; 1:16
7 Deuteronomy 31:9, 11-13; Nehemiah 8:2-3; Nehemiah 9:3-5
8 Deuteronomy 17:19, Revelation 1:3; John 5:39; Isaiah 34:16
9 Deuteronomy 6:6-9; Genesis 18:17, 19; Psalm 78:5-7
10 1 Corinthians 14:6, 9, 11-12, 15-16, 24, 27-28
11 Psalm 19:10; Nehemiah 8:3-10; Exodus 24:7; 2 Chronicles 34:27; Isaiah 66:2
12 2 Peter 1:19-21
13 Luke 24:45; 2 Corinthians 3:13-16
14 Deuteronomy 17:10, 20
15 Acts 17:11
16 Acts 8:30, 34; Luke 10:26-28
17 Psalm 1:2; 119:97
18 2 Chronicles 34:21
19 Proverbs 3:5; Deuteronomy 33:3
20 Proverbs 2:1-6; Psalm 119:18; Nehemiah 7:6, 8
21 1 Timothy 3:2, 6; Ephesians 4:8-11; Hosea 4:6; Malachi 2:7; 2 Corinthians 3:6
22 Jeremiah 14:15; Romans 10:15; Hebrews 5:4; 1 Corinthians 12:28-29; 1 Timothy 3:10; 4:14; 5:22

Q. 159. *How is the Word of God to be preached by those that are called thereunto?*

A. They that are called to labour in the ministry of the Word, are to preach sound doctrine,[1] diligently,[2] in season and out of season;[3] plainly,[4] not in the enticing words of man's wisdom, but in demonstration of the Spirit, and of power;[5] faithfully,[6] making known the whole counsel of God;[7] wisely,[8] applying themselves to the necessities and capacities of the hearers;[9] zealously,[10] with fervent love to God[11] and the souls of his people;[12] sincerely,[13] aiming at his glory,[14] and their conversion,[15] edification,[16] and salvation.[17]

Q. 160. *What is required of those that hear the Word preached?*

A. It is required of those that hear the Word preached, that they attend upon it with diligence,[18] preparation,[19] and prayer;[20] examine what they hear by the Scriptures;[21] receive the truth with faith,[22] love,[23] meekness,[24] and readiness of mind,[25] as the Word of God;[26]

---

1   Titus 2:1, 8
2   Acts 18:25
3   2 Timothy 4:2
4   1 Corinthians 14:19
5   1 Corinthians 2:4
6   Jeremiah 23:28; 1 Corinthians 4:1-2
7   Acts 20:27
8   Colossians 1:28; 2 Timothy 2:15
9   1 Corinthians 3:2; Hebrews 5:12-14; Luke 12:42
10 Acts 18:25
11 2 Corinthians 5:13-14; Philippians 1:15-17
12 Colossians 4:12; 2 Corinthians 12:15
13 2 Corinthians 2:17; 4:2
14 1 Thessalonians 2:4-6; John 7:18
15 1 Corinthians 9:19-22
16 2 Corinthians 12:19; Ephesians 4:12
17 1 Timothy 4:16; Acts 26:16-18
18 Proverbs 8:34
19 1 Peter 2:1-2; Luke 8:18
20 Psalm 119:18; Ephesians 6:18-19
21 Acts 17:11
22 Hebrews 4:2
23 2 Thessalonians 2:10
24 James 1:21
25 Acts 17:11
26 1 Thessalonians 2:13

meditate,[1] and confer of it;[2] hide it in their hearts,[3] and bring forth the fruit of it in their lives.[4]

Q. 161. *How do the sacraments become effectual means of salvation?*

A. The sacraments become effectual means of salvation, not by any power in themselves, or any virtue derived from the piety or intention of him by whom they are administered, but only by the working of the Holy Spirit, and the blessing of Christ, by whom they are instituted.[5]

Q. 162. *What is a sacrament?*

A. A sacrament is a holy ordinance instituted by Christ in his church,[6] to signify, seal, and exhibit[7] unto those that are within the covenant of grace,[8] the benefits of his mediation;[9] to strengthen and increase their faith, and all other graces;[10] to oblige them to obedience;[11] to testify and cherish their love and communion one with another;[12] and to distinguish them from those that are without.[13]

Q. 163. *What are the parts of a sacrament?*

A. The parts of the sacrament are two; the one an outward and sensible sign, used according to Christ's own appointment; the other an inward and spiritual grace thereby signified.[14]

Q. 164. *How many sacraments has Christ instituted in his church under the New Testament?*

A. Under the New Testament Christ has instituted in his church only two sacraments; baptism and the Lord's supper.[15]

Q. 165. *What is baptism?*

A. Baptism is a sacrament of the New Testament, wherein Christ has

---

1   Luke 9:44; Hebrews 2:1
2   Luke 24:14; Deuteronomy 6:6-7
3   Proverbs 2:1; Psalm 119:11
4   Luke 8:15; James 1:25
5   1 Peter 3:21;Acts 8:13 compared with verse 23; 1 Corinthians 3:6-7; 1 Corinthians 12:13
6   Genesis 17:7, 10; Exodus 12; Matthew 28:19; 26:26-28
7   Romans 4:11; 1 Corinthians 11:24-25
8   Romans 15:8; Exodus 12:48
9   Acts 2:38; 1 Corinthians 10:16
10 Romans 4:11; Galatians 3:27
11 Romans 6:3-4; 1 Corinthians 10:21
12 Ephesians 4:2-5; 1 Corinthians 12:13
13 Ephesians 2:11-12; Genesis 34:14
14 Matthew 3:11; 1 Peter 3:21; Romans 2:28-29
15 Matthew 28:19; 1 Corinthians 11:20, 23; Matthew 26:26-28

ordained the washing with water in the name of the Father, and of the Son, and of the Holy Spirit,[1] to be a sign and seal of ingrafting into himself,[2] of remission of sins by his blood,[3] and regeneration by his Spirit;[4] of adoption,[5] and resurrection unto everlasting life;[6] and whereby the parties baptised are solemnly admitted into the visible church,[7] and enter into an open and professed engagement to be wholly and only the Lord's.[8]

Q. 166. *Unto whom is baptism to be administered?*

A. Baptism is not to be administered to any that are out of the visible church, and so strangers from the covenant of promise, till they profess their faith in Christ, and obedience to him,[9] but infants descending from parents, either both, or but one of them, professing faith in Christ, and obedience to him, are in that respect within the covenant, and to be baptised.[10]

Q. 167. *How is our baptism to be improved by us?*

A. The needful but much neglected duty of improving our baptism, is to be performed by us all our life long, especially in the time of temptation, and when we are present at the administration of it to others;[11] by serious and thankful consideration of the nature of it, and of the ends for which Christ instituted it, the privileges and benefits conferred and sealed thereby, and our solemn vow made therein;[12] by being humbled for our sinful defilement, our falling short of, and walking contrary to, the grace of baptism, and our engagements;[13] by growing up to assurance of pardon of sin, and of all other blessings sealed to us in that sacrament;[14] by drawing strength from the death and resurrection of Christ, into whom we

---

1   Matthew 28:19
2   Galatians 3:27
3   Mark 1:4; Revelation 1:5
4   Titus 3:5; Ephesians 5:26
5   Galatians 3:26–27
6   1 Corinthians 15:29; Romans 6:5
7   1 Corinthians 12:13
8   Romans 6:4
9   Acts 8:36–37; Acts 2:38
10 Genesis 17:7, 9 compared with Galatians 3:9, 14 and with Colossians 2:11–12 and with Acts 2:38–39 and with Romans 4:11–12; 1 Corinthians 7:14; Matthew 28:19; Luke 18:15–16; Romans 11:16
11 Colossians 2:11–12; Romans 6:4, 6, 11
12 Romans 6:3–5
13 1 Corinthians 1:11–13; Romans 6:2–3
14 Romans 4:11–12; 1 Peter 3:21

are baptised, for the mortifying of sin, and quickening of grace;[1] and by endeavouring to live by faith,[2] to have our conversation in holiness and righteousness,[3] as those that have therein given up their names to Christ;[4] and to walk in brotherly love, as being baptised by the same Spirit into one body.[5]

Q. 168. *What is the Lord's supper?*

A. The Lord's supper is a sacrament of the New Testament,[6] wherein, by giving and receiving bread and wine according to the appointment of Jesus Christ, his death is showed forth; and they that worthily communicate feed upon his body and blood, to their spiritual nourishment and growth in grace;[7] have their union and communion with him confirmed;[8] testify and renew their thankfulness,[9] and engagement to God,[10] and their mutual love and fellowship each with the other, as members of the same mystical body.[11]

Q. 169. *How has Christ appointed bread and wine to be given and received in the sacrament of the Lord's supper?*

A. Christ has appointed the ministers of his Word, in the administration of this sacrament of the Lord's supper, to set apart the bread and wine from common use, by the word of institution, thanksgiving, and prayer; to take and break the bread, and to give both the bread and the wine to the communicants: who are, by the same appointment, to take and eat the bread, and to drink the wine, in thankful remembrance that the body of Christ was broken and given, and his blood shed, for them.[12]

Q. 170. *How do they that worthily communicate in the Lord's supper feed upon the body and blood of Christ therein?*

A. As the body and blood of Christ are not corporally or carnally

---

1 Romans 6:3–5
2 Galatians 3:26–27
3 Romans 6:22
4 Acts 2:38
5 1 Corinthians 12:13, 25–27
6 Luke 22:20
7 Matthew 26:26–28; 1 Corinthians 11:23–26
8 1 Corinthians 10:16
9 1 Corinthians 11:24
10 1 Corinthians 10:14–16, 21
11 1 Corinthians 10:17
12 1 Corinthians 11:23–24; Matthew 26:26–28; Mark 14:22–24; Luke 22:19–20

present in, with, or under the bread and wine in the Lord's supper,[1] and yet are spiritually present to the faith of the receiver, no less truly and really than the elements themselves are to their outward senses;[2] so they that worthily communicate in the sacrament of the Lord's supper, do therein feed upon the body and blood of Christ, not after a corporal and carnal, but in a spiritual manner; yet truly and really,[3] while by faith they receive and apply unto themselves Christ crucified, and all the benefits of his death.[4]

Q. 171. *How are they that receive the sacrament of the Lord's supper to prepare themselves before they come unto it?*

A. They that receive the sacrament of the Lord's supper are, before they come, to prepare themselves thereunto, by examining themselves[5] of their being in Christ,[6] of their sins and wants;[7] of the truth and measure of their knowledge,[8] faith,[9] repentance;[10] love to God and the brethren,[11] charity to all men,[12] forgiving those that have done them wrong;[13] of their desires after Christ,[14] and of their new obedience;[15] and by renewing the exercise of these graces,[16] by serious meditation,[17] and fervent prayer.[18]

Q. 172. *May one who doubts of his being in Christ, or of his due preparation, come to the Lord's supper?*

A. One who doubts of his being in Christ, or of his due preparation to the sacrament of the Lord's supper, may have true interest in Christ, though he be not yet assured thereof;[19] and in God's account

---

1   Acts 3:21
2   Matthew 26:26, 28
3   1 Corinthians 11:24–29
4   1 Corinthians 10:16
5   1 Corinthians 11:28
6   2 Corinthians 13:5
7   1 Corinthians 5:7 compared with Exodus 12:15
8   1 Corinthians 11:29
9   1 Corinthians 13:5; Matthew 26:28
10 Zechariah 12:10; 1 Corinthians 11:31
11 1 Corinthians 10:16–17; Acts 2:46–47
12 1 Corinthians 5:8; 11:18, 20
13 Matthew 5:23–24
14 Isaiah 55:1; John 7:37
15 1 Corinthians 5:7–8
16 1 Corinthians11:25–26, 28; Hebrews 10:21–22, 24; Psalm 26:6
17 1 Corinthians 11:24–25
18 2 Corinthians 30:18–19; Matthew 26:26
19 Isaiah 50:10; 1 John 5:13; Psalm 88; Psalm 77:1–12; Jonah 2:4, 7

has it, if he be duly affected with the apprehension of the want of it,[1] and un-feignedly desires to be found in Christ,[2] and to depart from iniquity:[3] in which case (because promises are made, and this sacrament is appointed, for the relief even of weak and doubting Christians)[4] he is to bewail his unbelief,[5] and labour to have his doubts resolved;[6] and, so doing, he may and ought to come to the Lord's supper, that he may be further strengthened.[7]

Q. 173. *May any who profess the faith, and desire to come to the Lord's supper, be kept from it?*

A. Such as are found to be ignorant or scandalous, notwithstanding their profession of the faith, and desire to come to the Lord's supper, may and ought to be kept from that sacrament, by the power which Christ has left in his church,[8] until they receive instruction, and manifest their reformation.[9]

Q. 174. *What is required of them that receive the sacrament of the Lord's supper in the time of the administration of it?*

A. It is required of them that receive the sacrament of the Lord's supper, that, during the time of the administration of it, with all holy reverence and attention they wait upon God in that ordinance,[10] diligently observe the sacramental elements and actions,[11] heedfully discern the Lord's body,[12] and affectionately meditate on his death and sufferings,[13] and thereby stir up themselves to a vigorous exercise of their graces;[14] in judging themselves,[15] and sorrowing for sin;[16] in earnest hungering and thirsting after Christ,[17] feeding on him by

---

1 Isaiah 54:7-10; Matthew 5:3-4; Psalm 31:22; 73:13, 22-23
2 Philippians 3:8-9; Psalm 10:17; 42:1-2, 5, 11
3 2 Timothy 2:19; Isaiah 50:10; Psalm 66:18-20
4 Isaiah 40:11, 29, 31; Matthew 11:28; 12:20; 26:28
5 Mark 9:24
6 Acts 2:37; 16:30
7 Romans 4:11; 1 Corinthians 11:28
8 1 Corinthians 11:27-34 compared with Matthew 7:6 and with 1 Corinthians 5 and with Jude 23 and with 1 Timothy 5:22
9 2 Corinthians 2:7
10 Leviticus 10:3; Hebrews 12:28; Psalm 5:7; 1 Corinthians 11:17, 26-27
11 Exodus 24:8 compared with Matthew 26:28
12 1 Corinthians 11:29
13 Luke 22:19
14 1 Corinthians 11:26; 10:3-5, 11, 14
15 1 Corinthians 11:31
16 Zechariah 12:10
17 Revelation 22:17

faith,[1] receiving of his fullness,[2] trusting in his merits,[3] rejoicing in his love,[4] giving thanks for his grace;[5] in renewing of their covenant with God,[6] and love to all the saints.[7]

Q. 175. *What is the duty of Christians, after they have received the sacrament of the Lord's supper?*

A. The duty of Christians, after they have received the sacrament of the Lord's supper, is seriously to consider how they have behaved themselves therein, and with what success;[8] if they find quickening [restoration] and comfort, to bless God for it,[9] beg the continuance of it,[10] watch against relapses,[11] fulfil their vows,[12] and encourage themselves to a frequent attendance on that ordinance:[13] but if they find no present benefit, more exactly to review their preparation to, and carriage at, the sacrament;[14] in both which, if they can approve themselves to God and their own consciences, they are to wait for the fruit of it in due time:[15] but, if they see they have failed in either, they are to be humbled,[16] and to attend upon it afterwards with more care and diligence.[17]

Q. 176. *Wherein do the sacraments of baptism and the Lord's supper agree?*

A. The sacraments of baptism and the Lord's supper agree, in that the author of both is God;[18] the spiritual part of both is Christ and his benefits;[19] both are seals of the same covenant,[20] are to be dispensed

---

1   John 6:35
2   John 1:16
3   Philippians 1:16
4   Psalm 63:4–5; 2 Chronicles 30:21
5   Psalm 22:26
6   Jeremiah 50:5; Psalm 50:5
7   Acts 2:42
8   Psalm 28:7; 85:8; 1 Corinthians 11:17, 3 0–31
9   2 Chronicles 30:21–23, 25–26; Acts 2:42, 46–47
10 Psalm 36:10; Song of Solomon 3:4; 1 Chronicles 29:18
11 1 Corinthians 10:3–5, 12
12 Psalm 50:14
13 1 Corinthians 11:25–26; Acts 2:42, 46
14 Song of Solomon 5:1–6; Ecclesiastes 5:1–6
15 Psalm 123:1–2; 42:5, 8; 43:3–5
16 2 Chronicles 30:18–19; Isaiah 1:16, 18
17 2 Corinthians 7:11; 1 Chronicles 15:12–14
18 Matthew 28:19; 1 Corinthians 11:23
19 Romans 6:3–4; 1 Corinthians 10:16
20 Romans 4:11; Colossians 2:12; Matthew 26:27–28

by ministers of the gospel, and by none other;[1] and to be continued in the church of Christ until his second coming.[2]

Q. 177. *Wherein do the sacraments of baptism and the Lord's supper differ?*

A. The sacraments of baptism and the Lord's supper differ, in that baptism is to be administered but once, with water, to be a sign and seal of our regeneration and ingrafting into Christ,[3] and that even to infants;[4] whereas the Lord's supper is to be administered often, in the elements of bread and wine, to represent and exhibit Christ as spiritual nourishment to the soul,[5] and to confirm our continuance and growth in him,[6] and that only to such as are of years and ability to examine themselves.[7]

Q. 178. *What is prayer?*

A. Prayer is an offering up of our desires unto God,[8] in the name of Christ,[9] by the help of his Spirit;[10] with confession of our sins,[11] and thankful acknowledgment of his mercies.[12]

Q. 179. *Are we to pray unto God only?*

A. God only being able to search the hearts,[13] hear the requests,[14] pardon the sins,[15] and fulfil the desires of all;[16] and only to be believed in,[17] and worshipped with religious worship;[18] prayer, which is a special part thereof,[19] is to be made by all to him alone,[20] and to none other.[21]

---

1 John 1:33; Matthew 28:19; 1 Corinthians 11:23; 4:1; Hebrews 5:4
2 Matthew 28:19–20; 1 Corinthians 11:26
3 Matthew 3:11; Titus 3:5; Galatians 3:27
4 Genesis 17:7, 9; Acts 2:38–39; 1 Corinthians 7:14
5 1 Corinthians 11:23–26
6 1 Corinthians 10:16
7 1 Corinthians 11:28–29
8 Psalm 62:8
9 John 16:23
10 Romans 8:26
11 Psalm 32:5–6; Daniel 9:4
12 Philippians 4:6
13 1 Kings 8:39; Acts 1:24; Romans 8:27
14 Psalm 65:2
15 Micah 7:18
16 Psalm 145:18–19
17 Romans 10:14
18 Matthew 4:10
19 1 Corinthians 1:2
20 Psalm 50:15
21 Romans 10:14

Q. 180. *What is it to pray in the name of Christ?*
A. To pray in the name of Christ is, in obedience to his command, and
in confidence on his promises, to ask mercy for his sake;[1] not by
bare mentioning of his name,[2] but by drawing our encouragement
to pray, and our boldness, strength, and hope of acceptance in
prayer, from Christ and his mediation.[3]

Q. 181. *Why are we to pray in the name of Christ?*
A. The sinfulness of man, and his distance from God by reason thereof,
being so great, as that we can have no access into his presence
without a mediator;[4] and there being none in heaven or earth
appointed to, or fit for, that glorious work but Christ alone,[5] we are
to pray in no other name but his only.[6]

Q. 182. *How does the Spirit help us to pray?*
A. We not knowing what to pray for as we ought, the Spirit helps our
infirmities, by enabling us to understand both for whom, and what,
and how prayer is to be made; and by working and quickening in
our hearts (although not in all persons, nor at all times, in the same
measure) those apprehensions, affections, and graces which are
requisite for the right performance of that duty.[7]

Q. 183. *For whom are we to pray?*
A. We are to pray for the whole church of Christ upon earth;[8] for
magistrates,[9] and ministers;[10] for ourselves,[11] our brethren,[12] yea,
our enemies;[13] and for all sorts of men living,[14] or that shall live

1 John 14:13–14; John 16:24; Daniel 9:17
2 Matthew 7:21
3 Hebrews 4:14–16; 1 John 5:13–15
4 John 14:6; Isaiah 59:2; Ephesians 3:12
5 John 6:27; Hebrews 7:25–27; 1 Timothy 2:5
6 Colossians 3:17; Hebrews 13:15
7 Romans 8:26–27; Psalm 10:17; Zechariah 12:10
8 Ephesians 6:18; Psalm 28:9
9 1 Timothy 2:1–2
10 Colossians 4:3
11 Genesis 32:11
12 James 5:16
13 Matthew 5:44
14 1 Timothy 2:1–2

hereafter;[1] but not for the dead,[2] nor for those that are known to have sinned the sin unto death.[3]

Q. 184. *For what things are we to pray?*

A. We are to pray for all things tending to the glory of God,[4] the welfare of the church,[5] our own[6] or others', good;[7] but not for anything that is unlawful.[8]

Q. 185. *How are we to pray?*

A. We are to pray with an awful apprehension of the majesty of God,[9] and deep sense of our own unworthiness,[10] necessities,[11] and sins;[12] with penitent,[13] thankful,[14] and enlarged hearts;[15] with understanding,[16] faith,[17] sincerity,[18] fervency,[19] love,[20] and perseverance,[21] waiting upon him,[22] with humble submission to his will.[23]

Q. 186. *What rule has God given for our direction in the duty of prayer?*

A. The whole Word of God is of use to direct us in the duty of prayer;[24] but the special rule of direction is that form of prayer which our Saviour Christ taught his disciples, commonly called The Lord's Prayer.[25]

---

1   John 17:20; 2 Samuel 7:29
2   2 Samuel 12:21–23
3   1 John 5:16
4   Matthew 6:9
5   Psalm 51:18; 122:6
6   Matthew 7:11
7   Psalm 125:4
8   1 John 5:14
9   Ecclesiastes 5:1
10 Genesis 18:27; 32:10
11 Luke 15:17–19
12 Luke 18:13–14
13 Psalm 51:17
14 Philippians 4:6
15 1 Samuel 1:15; 2:1
16 1 Corinthians 14:15
17 Mark 11:24; James 1:6
18 Psalm 145:18; Psalm 17:1
19 James 5:16
20 1 Timothy 2:8
21 Ephesians 6:18
22 Micah 7:7
23 Matthew 26:39
24 1 John 5:14
25 Matthew 6:9–13; Luke 11:2–4

Q. 187. *How is the Lord's Prayer to be used?*
A. The Lord's Prayer is not only for direction, as a pattern, according to which we are to make other prayers; but may also be used as a prayer, so that it be done with understanding, faith, reverence, and other graces necessary to the right performance of the duty of prayer.[1]

Q. 188. *Of how many parts does the Lord's Prayer consist?*
A. The Lord's Prayer consists of three parts; a preface, petitions, and a conclusion.

Q. 189. *What does the preface of the Lord's Prayer teach us?*
A. The preface of the Lord's Prayer (contained in these words, Our Father in heaven,)[2] teaches us, when we pray, to draw near to God with confidence of his fatherly goodness, and our interest therein;[3] with reverence, and all other childlike dispositions,[4] heavenly affections,[5] and due apprehensions of his sovereign power, majesty, and gracious condescension:[6] as also, to pray with and for others.[7]

Q. 190. *What do we pray for in the first petition?*
A. In the first petition, (which is, Hallowed be your name,)[8] acknowledging the utter inability and indisposition that is in ourselves and all men to honour God aright,[9] we pray, that God would by his grace enable and incline us and others to know, to acknowledge, and highly to esteem him,[10] his titles,[11] attributes,[12] ordinances, Word,[13] works, and whatsoever he is pleased to make himself known by;[14] and to glorify him in thought, word,[15] and

---

1   Matthew 6:9 compared with Luke 11:2
2   Matthew 6:9
3   Luke 11:13; Romans 8:15
4   Isaiah 64:9
5   Psalm 123:1; Lamentations 3:41
6   Isaiah 63:15–16; Nehemiah 1:4–6
7   Acts 12:5
8   Matthew 6:9
9   2 Corinthians 3:5; Psalm 51:15
10 Psalm 67:2–3
11 Psalm 83:18
12 Psalm 86:10–13, 15
13 2 Thessalonians 3:1; Psalm 147:19–20; 138:1–3; 2 Corinthians 2:14–15
14 Psalm 145; 8
15 Psalm 103:1; 19:14

deed:[1] that he would prevent and remove atheism,[2] ignorance,[3] idolatry,[4] profaneness,[5] and whatsoever is dishonourable to him;[6] and, by his over-ruling providence, direct and dispose of all things to his own glory.[7]

Q. 191. *What do we pray for in the second petition?*

A. In the second petition, (which is, Your kingdom come,)[8] acknowledging ourselves and all mankind to be by nature under the dominion of sin and Satan,[9] we pray, that the kingdom of sin and Satan may be destroyed,[10] the gospel propagated throughout the world,[11] the Jews called,[12] the fullness of the Gentiles brought in;[13] the church furnished with all gospel-officers and ordinances,[14] purged from corruption,[15] countenanced and maintained by the civil magistrate:[16] that the ordinances of Christ may be purely dispensed, and made effectual to the converting of those that are yet in their sins, and the confirming, comforting, and building up of those that are already converted:[17] that Christ would rule in our hearts here,[18] and hasten the time of his second coming, and our reigning with him forever:[19] and that he would be pleased so to exercise the kingdom of his power in all the world, as may best conduce to these ends.[20]

Q. 192. *What do we pray for in the third petition?*

A. In the third petition, (which is, Your will be done, on earth as it

---

1   Philippians 1:9, 11
2   Psalm 67:1–4
3   Ephesians 1:17–18
4   Psalm 97:7
5   Psalm 74:18, 22–23
6   2 Kings 19:15–16
7   2 Chronicles 20:6, 10–12; Psalm 83; 140:4, 8
8   Matthew 6:10
9   Ephesians 2:2–3
10   Psalm 68:1, 18; Revelation 12:10–11
11   2 Thessalonians 3:1
12   Romans 10:1
13   John 17:9, 20; Romans 11:25–26; Psalm 67
14   Matthew 9:38; 2 Thessalonians 3:1
15   Malachi 1:11; Zephaniah 3:9
16   1 Timothy 2:1–2
17   Acts 4:29–30; Ephesians 6:18–20; Romans 15:29–30, 32; 2 Thessalonians 1:11; 2:16–17
18   Ephesians 3:14–20
19   Revelation 22:20
20   Isaiah 64:1–2; Revelation 4:8–11

is in heaven,)[1] acknowledging, that by nature we and all men are not only utterly unable and unwilling to know and do the will of God,[2] but prone to rebel against his Word,[3] to repine [fret] and murmur against his providence,[4] and wholly inclined to do the will of the flesh, and of the devil:[5] we pray, that God would by his Spirit take away from ourselves and others all blindness,[6] weakness,[7] indisposedness,[8] and perverseness of heart;[9] and by his grace make us able and willing to know, do, and submit to his will in all things,[10] with humility,[11] cheerfulness,[12] faithfulness,[13] diligence,[14] zeal,[15] sincerity,[16] and constancy,[17] as the angels do in heaven.[18]

Q. 193. *What do we pray for in the fourth petition?*
A. In the fourth petition,(which is, Give us this day our daily bread,)[19] acknowledging, that in Adam, and by our own sin, we have forfeited our right to all the outward blessings of this life, and deserve to be wholly deprived of them by God, and to have them cursed to us in the use of them;[20] and that neither they of themselves are able to sustain us,[21] nor we to merit,[22] or by our own industry to procure [obtain] them;[23] but prone to desire,[24] get,[25] and use them

---

1   Matthew 6:10
2   Romans 7:18; Job 21:14; 1 Corinthians 2:14
3   Romans 8:7
4   Exodus 17:7; Numbers 14:2
5   Ephesians 2:2
6   Ephesians 1:17-18
7   Ephesians 3:16
8   Matthew 26:40-41
9   Jeremiah 31:18-19
10 Psalm 119:1, 8, 35-36; Acts 21:14
11 Micah 6:8
12 Psalm 100:2; Job 1:21; 2 Samuel 15:25-26
13 Isaiah 38:3
14 Psalm 119:4-5
15 Romans 12:11
16 Psalm 119:80
17 Psalm 119:112
18 Isaiah 6:2-3; Psalm 103:20-21; Matthew 18:10
19 Matthew 6:11
20 Genesis 2:17; 3:17; Romans 8:20-22; Jeremiah 5:25; Deuteronomy 28:15-68
21 Deuteronomy 8:3
22 Genesis 32:10
23 Deuteronomy 8:17-18
24 Jeremiah 6:13; Mark 7:21-22
25 Hosea 12:7

unlawfully:[1] we pray for ourselves and others, that both they and we, waiting upon the providence of God from day to day in the use of lawful means, may, of his free gift, and as to his fatherly wisdom shall seem best, enjoy a competent portion of them;[2] and have the same continued and blessed unto us in our holy and comfortable use of them,[3] and contentment in them;[4] and be kept from all things that are contrary to our temporal support and comfort.[5]

Q. 194. *What do we pray for in the fifth petition?*

A. In the fifth petition, (which is, Forgive us our debts, as we also have forgiven our debtors,)[6] acknowledging, that we and all others are guilty both of original and actual sin, and thereby become debtors to the justice of God; and that neither we, nor any other creature, can make the least satisfaction for that debt:[7] we pray for ourselves and others, that God of his free grace would, through the obedience and satisfaction of Christ, apprehended and applied by faith, acquit us both from the guilt and punishment of sin,[8] accept us in his Beloved;[9] continue his favour and grace to us,[10] pardon our daily failings,[11] and fill us with peace and joy, in giving us daily more and more assurance of forgiveness;[12] which we are the rather emboldened to ask, and encouraged to expect, when we have this testimony in ourselves, that we from the heart forgive others their offenses.[13]

Q. 195. *What do we pray for in the sixth petition?*

A. In the sixth petition, (which is, And lead us not into temptation, but deliver us from evil,)[14] acknowledging, that the most wise, righteous, and gracious God, for divers [various] holy and just ends, may so order things, that we may be assaulted, foiled, and for a time led

---

1   James 4:3
2   Genesis 43:12–14; 28:20; Ephesians 4:28; 2 Thessalonians 3:11–12; Philippians 4:6
3   1 Timothy 4:3–5
4   1 Timothy 6:6–8
5   Proverbs 30:8–9
6   Matthew 6:12
7   Romans 3:9–22; Matthew 18:24–25; Psalm 130:3–4
8   Romans 3:24–26; Hebrews 9:22
9   Ephesians 1:6–7
10 2 Peter 1:2
11 Hosea 14:2; Jeremiah 14:7
12 Romans 15:13; Psalm 51:7–10, 12
13 Luke 11:4; Matthew 6:14–15; 18:35
14 Matthew 6:13

captive by temptations;[1] that Satan,[2] the world,[3] and the flesh, are ready powerfully to draw us aside, and ensnare us;[4] and that we, even after the pardon of our sins, by reason of our corruption,[5] weakness, and want of watchfulness,[6] are not only subject to be tempted, and forward to expose ourselves unto temptations,[7] but also of ourselves unable and unwilling to resist them, to recover out of them, and to improve them;[8] and worthy to be left under the power of them:[9] we pray, that God would so overrule the world and all in it,[10] subdue the flesh,[11] and restrain Satan,[12] order all things,[13] bestow and bless all means of grace,[14] and quicken [awaken] us to watchfulness in the use of them, that we and all his people may by his providence be kept from being tempted to sin;[15] or, if tempted, that by his Spirit we may be powerfully supported and enabled to stand in the hour of temptation;[16] or when fallen, raised again and recovered out of it,[17] and have a sanctified use and improvement thereof:[18] that our sanctification and salvation may be perfected,[19] Satan trodden under our feet,[20] and we fully freed from sin, temptation, and all evil, forever.[21]

Q. 196. *What does the conclusion of the Lord's Prayer teach us?*

A. The conclusion of the Lord's Prayer, (which is, For yours is the kingdom, and the power, and the glory, for ever. Amen.)[22] teaches

---

1   2 Chronicles 32:31
2   1 Chronicles 21:1
3   Luke 21:34; Mark 4:19
4   James 1:14
5   Galatians 5:17
6   Matthew 26:41
7   Matthew 26:69–72; Galatians 2:11–14; 2 Chronicles 18:3 compared with 2 Chronicles 19:2
8   Romans 7:23–24; 1 Chronicles 21:1–4; 2 Chronicles 16:7–10
9   Psalm 81:11–12
10 John 17:15
11 Psalm 51:10; 119:133
12 2 Corinthians 12:7–8
13 1 Corinthians 10:12–13
14 Hebrews 13:20–21
15 Matthew 26:41; Psalm 19:13
16 Ephesians 3:14–17; 1 Thessalonians 3:13; Jude 24
17 Psalm 51:12
18 1 Peter 5:8–10
19 2 Corinthians 13:7, 9
20 Romans 16:20; Zechariah 3:2; Luke 22:31–32
21 John 17:15; 1 Thessalonians 5:23
22 Matthew 6:13

us to enforce our petitions with arguments,[1] which are to be taken, not from any worthiness in ourselves, or in any other creature, but from God;[2] and with our prayers to join praises,[3] ascribing to God alone eternal sovereignty, omnipotence, and glorious excellency;[4] in regard whereof, as he is able and willing to help us,[5] so we by faith are emboldened to plead with him that he would,[6] and quietly to rely upon him, that he will fulfil our requests.[7] And, to testify this our desire and assurance, we say, Amen.[8]

---

1   Romans 15:30
2   Daniel 9:4, 7–9, 16–19
3   Philippians 4:6
4   1 Chronicles 29:10–13
5   Ephesians 3:20–21; Luke 11:13
6   2 Chronicles 20:6, 11
7   2 Chronicles 14:11
8   1 Corinthians 14:16; Revelation 22:20–21

The Westminster Shorter Catechism in Modern English

Q. 1. *What is the chief end of man?*
A. Man's chief end is to glorify God,[1] and to enjoy him forever.[2]

Q. 2. *What rule has God given to direct us how we may glorify and enjoy him?*
A. The Word of God, which is contained in the Scriptures of the Old and New Testaments,[3] is the only rule to direct us how we may glorify and enjoy him.[4]

Q. 3. *What do the Scriptures principally teach?*
A. The Scriptures principally teach, what man is to believe concerning God, and what duty God requires of man.[5]

Q. 4. *What is God?*
A. God is a Spirit,[6] infinite,[7] eternal,[8] and unchangeable,[9] in his being,[10] wisdom,[11] power,[12] holiness,[13] justice, goodness, and truth.[14]

---

1   1 Corinthians 10:31
2   Psalms 73:25–26
3   Ephesians 2:20; 2 Timothy 3:16
4   1 John 1:3
5   2 Timothy 1:13
6   John 4:24
7   Job 11:7
8   Psalms 90:2
9   James 1:17
10 Exodus 3:14
11 Psalms 147:5
12 Revelation 4:8
13 Revelation 15:4
14 Exodus 34:6–7

Q. 5. *Are there more Gods than one?*
A. There is only one,[1] the living and true God.[2]

Q. 6. *How many persons are there in the Godhead?*
A. There are three persons in the Godhead: the Father, the Son, and the Holy Spirit;[3] and these three are one God, the same in substance, equal in power and glory.[4]

Q. 7. *What are the decrees of God?*
A. The decrees of God are, his eternal purpose, according to the counsel of his will, whereby, for his own glory, he has foreordained whatsoever comes to pass.[5]

Q. 8. *How does God execute his decrees?*
A. God executes his decrees in the works of creation[6] and providence.[7]

Q. 9. *What is the work of creation?*
A. The work of creation is, God's making all things out of nothing,[8] by the word of his power,[9] in the space of six days, and all very good.[10]

Q. 10. *How did God create man?*
A. God created man male and female, after his own image,[11] in knowledge, righteousness, and holiness,[12] with dominion over the creatures.[13]

Q. 11. *What are God's works of providence?*
A. God's works of providence are, his most holy,[14] wise,[15] and powerful preserving[16] and governing all his creatures, and all their actions.[17]

---

1 Deuteronomy 6:4
2 Jeremiah 10:10
3 Matthew 28:19
4 1 John 5:7
5 Ephesians 1:11–12
6 Revelation 4:11
7 Daniel 4:35
8 Genesis 1:1
9 Hebrews 11:3
10 Genesis 1:31
11 Genesis 1:27
12 Colossians 3:10; Ephesians 4:24
13 Genesis 1:28
14 Psalms 145:17
15 Isaiah 28:29
16 Hebrews 1:3
17 Psalm 103:19; Matthew 10:29

Q. 12. *What special act of providence did God exercise towards man in the estate in which he was created?*

A. When God had created man, he entered into a covenant of life with him, upon condition of perfect obedience;[1] forbidding him to eat of the tree of the knowledge of good and evil, upon the pain of death.[2]

Q. 13. *Did our first parents continue in the estate in which they were created?*

A. Our first parents, being left to the freedom of their own will, fell from the estate in which they were created, by sinning against God.[3]

Q. 14. *What is sin?*

A. Sin is any lack of conformity unto, or transgression of, the law of God.[4]

Q. 15. *What was the sin whereby our first parents fell from the estate wherein they were created?*

A. The sin whereby our first parents fell from the estate wherein they were created, was their eating the forbidden fruit.[5]

Q. 16. *Did all mankind fall in Adam's first transgression?*

A. The covenant being made with Adam, not only for himself, but for his posterity;[6] all mankind, descending from him by natural birth, sinned in him, and fell with him, in his first transgression.[7]

Q. 17. *Into what estate did the fall bring mankind?*

A. The fall brought mankind into an estate of sin and misery.[8]

Q. 18. *Wherein consists the sinfulness of that estate into which man fell?*

A. The sinfulness of that estate into which man fell, consists in the guilt of Adam's first sin,[9] the lack of original righteousness,[10] and the

---

1   Galatians 3:12
2   Genesis 2:17
3   Ecclesiastes 7:29
4   1 John 3:4
5   Genesis 3:6–8
6   Genesis 1:28; 2:16–17
7   Romans 5:18
8   Romans 5:12
9   Romans 5:19
10   Romans 3:10

corruption of his whole nature, which is commonly called Original Sin;[1] together with all actual transgressions which proceed from it.[2]

Q. 19. *What is the misery of that estate into which man fell?*

A. All mankind by their fall lost communion with God,[3] are under his wrath and curse,[4] and so made liable to all the miseries of this life, to death itself, and to the pains of hell forever.[5]

Q. 20. *Did God leave all mankind to perish in the estate of sin and misery?*

A. God, having out of his mere good pleasure, from all eternity, elected some to everlasting life,[6] did enter into a covenant of grace to deliver them out of the estate of sin and misery, and to bring them into an estate of salvation by a Redeemer.[7]

Q. 21. *Who is the Redeemer of God's elect?*

A. The only Redeemer of God's elect is the Lord Jesus Christ,[8] who, being the eternal Son of God, became man,[9] and so was, and continues to be, God and man in two distinct natures, and one person,[10] forever.[11]

Q. 22. *How did Christ, being the Son of God, become man?*

A. Christ, the Son of God, became man, by taking to himself a true body,[12] and a reasonable soul,[13] being conceived by the power of the Holy Spirit, in the womb of the Virgin Mary, and born of her,[14] yet without sin.[15]

Q. 23. *What offices does Christ execute as our Redeemer?*

A. Christ, as our Redeemer, executes the offices of a prophet,[16] of

---

1   Ephesians 2:1; Psalms 51:5
2   Matthew 15:19-20
3   Genesis 3:8, 24
4   Ephesians 2:3; Galatians 3:10
5   Romans 6:23; Matthew 25:41
6   Ephesians 1:4
7   Romans 3:21-22
8   1 Timothy 2:5
9   John 1:14
10 Romans 9:5
11 Hebrews 7:24
12 Hebrews 2:14
13 Matthew 26:38
14 Luke 1:31, 35
15 Hebrews 7:26
16 Acts 3:22

a priest,[1] and of a king,[2] both in his estate of humiliation and exaltation.

Q. 24. *How does Christ execute the office of a prophet?*

A. Christ executes the office of a prophet, in revealing to us,[3] by his Word[4] and Spirit,[5] the will of God for our salvation.

Q. 25. *How does Christ execute the office of a priest?*

A. Christ executes the office of a priest, in his once offering up of himself a sacrifice to satisfy divine justice,[6] and reconcile us to God,[7] and in making continual intercession for us.[8]

Q. 26. *How does Christ execute the office of a king?*

A. Christ executes the office of a king, in subduing us to himself,[9] in ruling and defending us,[10] and in restraining and conquering all his and our enemies.[11]

Q. 27. *Wherein did Christ's humiliation consist?*

A. Christ's humiliation consisted in his being born, and that in a low condition,[12] made under the law,[13] undergoing the miseries of this life,[14] the wrath of God,[15] and the cursed death of the cross;[16] in being buried, and continuing under the power of death for a time.[17]

Q. 28. *Wherein consists Christ's exaltation?*

A. Christ's exaltation consists in his rising again from the dead on the

---

1   Hebrews 5:6
2   Psalm 2:6
3   John 1:18
4   John 20:31
5   John 14:26
6   Hebrews 9:28
7   Hebrews 2:17
8   Hebrews 7:25
9   Psalms 110:3
10   Isaiah 33:22
11   1 Corinthians 15:25
12   Luke 2:7
13   Galatians 4:4
14   Isaiah 53:3
15   Matthew 27:46
16   Philippians 2:8
17   Matthew 12:40

third day,[1] in ascending up into heaven, in sitting at the right hand of God the Father,[2] and in coming to judge the world at the last day.[3]

Q. 29. *How are we made partakers of the redemption purchased by Christ?*
A. We are made partakers of the redemption purchased by Christ, by the effectual application of it to us[4] by his Holy Spirit.[5]

Q. 30. *How does the Spirit apply to us the redemption purchased by Christ?*
A. The Spirit applies to us the redemption purchased by Christ, by working faith in us,[6] and thereby uniting us to Christ in our effectual calling.[7]

Q. 31. *What is effectual calling?*
A. Effectual calling is the work of God's Spirit,[8] whereby, convincing us of our sin and misery,[9] enlightening our minds in the knowledge of Christ,[10] and renewing our wills,[11] he does persuade and enable us to embrace Jesus Christ, freely offered to us in the gospel.[12]

Q. 32. *What benefits do they that are effectually called partake of in this life?*
A. They that are effectually called do in this life partake of justification,[13] adoption,[14] and sanctification, and the several benefits which in this life do either accompany or flow from them.[15]

Q. 33. *What is justification?*
A. Justification is an act of God's free grace, wherein he pardons all

---

1   1 Corinthians 15:4
2   Mark 16:19
3   Acts 17:31
4   John 1:12
5   Titus 3:5–6
6   Ephesians 2:8
7   1 Corinthians 1:9; Ephesians 3:17
8   2 Timothy 1:9
9   Acts 2:37
10 Acts 26:18
11 Ezekiel 36:26–27
12 John 6:44–45
13 Romans 8:30
14 Ephesians 1:5
15 1 Corinthians 1:30

our sins,[1] and accepts us as righteous in His sight,[2] only for the righteousness of Christ imputed to us,[3] and received by faith alone.[4]

Q. 34. *What is adoption?*

A. Adoption is an act of God's free grace,[5] whereby we are received into the number, and have a right to all the privileges of the sons of God.[6]

Q. 35. *What is sanctification?*

A. Sanctification is the work of God's free grace,[7] whereby we are renewed in the whole man after the image of God,[8] and are enabled more and more to die unto sin, and live unto righteousness.[9]

Q. 36. *What are the benefits which in this life do accompany or flow from justification, adoption, and sanctification?*

A. The benefits which in this life do accompany or flow from justification, adoption, and sanctification, are, assurance of God's love, peace of conscience, joy in the Holy Spirit,[10] increase of grace,[11] and perseverance therein to the end.[12]

Q. 37. *What benefits do believers receive from Christ at death?*

A. The souls of believers are at their death made perfect in holiness,[13] and do immediately pass into glory;[14] and their bodies, being still united to Christ,[15] do rest in their graves[16] until the resurrection.[17]

Q. 38. *What benefits do believers receive from Christ at the resurrection?*

A. At the resurrection, believers, being raised up in glory,[18] shall be

---

1   Ephesians 1:17
2   2 Corinthians 5:21
3   Romans 5:19
4   Galatians 2:16
5   1 John 3:1
6   John 1:12; Romans 8:17
7   2 Thessalonians 2:13
8   Ephesians 4:24,
9   Romans 8:1
10 Romans 5:1-2, 5
11 Proverbs 4:18
12 1 John 5:13
13 Hebrews 12:23
14 Philippians 1:23
15 1 Thessalonians 4:14
16 Isaiah 57:2
17 Job 19:26
18 1 Corinthians 15:43

openly acknowledged and acquitted in the day of judgment,[1] and made perfectly blessed in the full enjoying of God[2] to all eternity.[3]

Q. 39. *What is the duty which God requires of man?*
A. The duty which God requires of man, is obedience to his revealed will.[4]

Q. 40. *What did God at first reveal to man for the rule of his obedience?*
A. The rule which God at first revealed to man for his obedience, was the moral law.[5]

Q. 41. *Where is the moral law summarized?*
A. The moral law is summarized in the Ten Commandments.[6]

Q. 42. *What is the sum of the Ten Commandments?*
A. The sum of the Ten Commandments is, to love the Lord our God with all our heart, with all our soul, with all our strength, and with all our mind; and our neighbor as ourselves.[7]

Q. 43. *What is the preface to the Ten Commandments?*
A. The preface to the Ten Commandments is in these words, I am the Lord your God, who brought you out of the land of Egypt, out of the house of slavery.[8]

Q. 44. *What does the preface to the Ten Commandments teach us?*
A. The preface to the Ten Commandments teaches us, that because God is the Lord, and our God, and Redeemer, therefore we are bound to keep all his commandments.[9]

Q. 45. *Which is the first commandment?*
A. The first commandment is, You shall have no other gods before me.

Q. 46. *What is required in the first commandment?*
A. The first commandment requires us to know[10] and acknowledge God

---

1   Matthew 10:32
2   1 John 3:2
3   1 Thessalonians 4:17
4   Micah 6:8
5   Romans 2:14–15
6   Deuteronomy 10:4; Matthew 19:17
7   Matthew 22:37–40
8   Exodus 20:2
9   Deuteronomy 11:1; Luke 1:74–75
10 1 Chronicles 28:9

to be the only true God, and our God;[1] and to worship and glorify him accordingly.[2]

Q. 47. *What is forbidden in the first commandment?*

A. The first commandment forbids the denying,[3] or not worshipping and glorifying, the true God as God,[4] and our God;[5] and the giving of that worship and glory to any other, which is due to him alone.[6]

Q. 48. *What are we specially taught by these words 'before me' in the first commandment?*

A. These words before me in the first commandment teach us, that God, who sees all things, takes notice of, and is much displeased with, the sin of having any other god.[7]

Q. 49. *Which is the second commandment?*

A. The second commandment is, You shall not make for yourself a carved image, or any likeness of anything that is in heaven above, or that is in the earth beneath, or that is in the water under the earth. You shall not bow down to them nor serve them; for I the LORD your God am a jealous God, visiting the iniquity of the fathers on the children to the third and the fourth generation of those who hate me; and showing steadfast love to thousands of those who love me and keep my commandments.

Q. 50. *What is required in the second commandment?*

A. The second commandment requires the receiving, observing,[8] and keeping pure and entire, all such religious worship and ordinances as God has appointed in his Word.[9]

Q. 51. *What is forbidden in the second commandment?*

A. The second commandment forbids the worshipping of God by images,[10] or any other way not appointed in his Word.[11]

---

1   Deuteronomy 26:17
2   Matthew 4:10
3   Psalms 14:1
4   Romans 1:20–21
5   Psalms 81:11
6   Romans 1:25
7   Psalms 44:20–21
8   Deuteronomy 32:46; Matthew 28:20
9   Deuteronomy 12:32
10 Deuteronomy 4:15–16
11 Colossians 2:18

Q. 52. *What are the reasons annexed to the second commandment?*
A. The reasons annexed to the second commandment are, God's sovereignty over us,[1] his propriety in us,[2] and the zeal he has to his own worship.[3]

Q. 53. *Which is the third commandment?*
A. The third commandment is, You shall not take the name of the Lord your God in vain, for the Lord will not hold him guiltless who takes his name in vain.

Q. 54. *What is required in the third commandment?*
A. The third commandment requires the holy and reverent use of God's names,[4] titles, attributes,[5] ordinances,[6] Word,[7] and works.[8]

Q. 55. *What is forbidden in the third commandment?*
A. The third commandment forbids all profaning or abusing of anything whereby God makes himself known.[9]

Q. 56. *What is the reason annexed to the third commandment?*
A. The reason annexed to the third commandment is, that however the breakers of this commandment may escape punishment from men, yet the Lord our God will not let them escape his righteous judgment.[10]

Q. 57. *Which is the fourth commandment?*
A. The fourth commandment is, Remember the Sabbath day, to keep it holy. Six days you shall labour, and do all your work, but the seventh day is a Sabbath to the LORD your God. On it you shall not do any work, you, nor your son, nor your daughter, your male servant, nor your female servant, nor your livestock, nor the sojourner who is within your gates. For in six days the LORD made heaven and earth, the sea, and all that is in them, and rested on the seventh day. Therefore the LORD blessed the Sabbath day and made it holy.

---

1   Psalms 95:2–3
2   Psalms 45:11
3   Exodus 34:14
4   Psalms 29:2
5   Revelation 15:3–4
6   Ecclesiastes 5:1
7   Psalms 138:2
8   Job 36:24
9   Malachi 2:2
10 Deuteronomy 28:58–59

Q. 58. *What is required in the fourth commandment?*

A. The fourth commandment requires the keeping holy to God such set times as he has appointed in his Word; expressly one whole day in seven, to be a holy Sabbath to himself.[1]

Q. 59. *Which day of the seven has God appointed to be the weekly Sabbath?*

A. From the beginning of the world to the resurrection of Christ, God appointed the seventh day of the week to be the weekly Sabbath;[2] and the first day of the week ever since, to continue to the end of the world, which is the Christian Sabbath.[3]

Q. 60. *How is the Sabbath to be sanctified?*

A. The sabbath is to be sanctified by a holy resting all that day, even from such worldly employments and recreations as are lawful on other days;[4] and spending the whole time in the public and private exercises of God's worship,[5] except so much as is to be taken up in the works of necessity and mercy.[6]

Q. 61. *What is forbidden in the fourth commandment?*

A. The fourth commandment forbids the omission, or careless performance of the duties required,[7] and the profaning the day by idleness, or doing that which is in itself sinful,[8] or by unnecessary thoughts, words, or works, about our worldly employments or recreations.[9]

Q. 62. *What are the reasons annexed to the fourth commandment?*

A. The reasons annexed to the fourth commandment are, God's allowing us six days of the week for our own employments,[10] his challenging a special propriety in the seventh,[11] his own example,[12] and his blessing the Sabbath day.[13]

---

1   Leviticus 19:30; Deuteronomy 5:12
2   Genesis 2:3
3   Acts 20:7; Revelation 1:10
4   Leviticus 23:3
5   Psalm 92:1–2
6   Matthew 12:11–12
7   Malachi 1:13
8   Ezekiel 23:38
9   Isaiah 58:13
10 Exodus 31:15–16
11 Leviticus 23:3
12 Exodus 31:17
13 Genesis 2:3

Q. 63. *Which is the fifth commandment?*
A. The fifth commandment is, Honour your father and your mother, that your days may be long in the land that the LORD your God is giving you.

Q. 64. *What is required in the fifth commandment?*
A. The fifth commandment requires the preserving the honour, and performing the duties, belonging to everyone in their several places and relations, as superiors,[1] inferiors,[2] or equals.[3]

Q. 65. *What is forbidden in the fifth commandment?*
A. The fifth commandment forbids the neglecting of, or doing anything against, the honour and duty which belongs to everyone in their several places and relations.[4]

Q. 66. *What is the reason annexed to the fifth commandment?*
A. The reason annexed to the fifth commandment is, a promise of long life and prosperity (as far as it shall serve for God's glory and their own good) to all such as keep this commandment.[5]

Q. 67. *Which is the sixth commandment?*
A. The sixth commandment is, You shall not murder.

Q. 68. *What is required in the sixth commandment?*
A. The sixth commandment requires all lawful endeavors to preserve our own life,[6] and the life of others.[7]

Q. 69. *What is forbidden in the sixth commandment?*
A. The sixth commandment forbids the taking away of our own life,[8] or the life of our neighbour,[9] unjustly, or whatsoever is related thereunto.[10]

Q. 70. *Which is the seventh commandment?*
A. The seventh commandment is, You shall not commit adultery.

---

1 Ephesians 5:21–22; 6:1, 5; Romans 13:1
2 1 Peter 3:16; Acts 25:10
3 Romans 12:10
4 Romans 13:7–8
5 Ephesians 6:2–3
6 Ephesians 5:28–29
7 Psalm 82:3–4; Job 29:13
8 Acts 16:28
9 Genesis 9:6
10 Proverbs 24:11–12

Q. 71. *What is required in the seventh commandment?*
A. The seventh commandment requires the preservation of our own[1] and our neighbour's chastity,[2] in heart,[3] speech,[4] and behaviour.[5]

Q. 72. *What is forbidden in the seventh commandment?*
A. The seventh commandment forbids all unchaste thoughts,[6] words,[7] and actions.[8]

Q. 73. *Which is the eighth commandment?*
A. The eighth commandment is, You shall not steal.

Q. 74. *What is required in the eighth commandment?*
A. The eighth commandment requires the lawful procuring [obtaining] and furthering the wealth and outward estate of ourselves[9] and others.[10]

Q. 75. *What is forbidden in the eighth commandment?*
A. The eighth commandment forbids whatsoever does, or may, unjustly hinder our own,[11] or our neighbour's wealth or outward estate.[12]

Q. 76. *Which is the ninth commandment?*
A. The ninth commandment is, You shall not bear false witness against your neighbour.

Q. 77. *What is required in the ninth commandment?*
A. The ninth commandment requires the maintaining and promoting of truth between man and man,[13] and of our own[14] and our neighbour's good name,[15] especially in witness-bearing.[16]

---

1 1 Thessalonians 4:4
2 Ephesians 5:11-12
3 2 Timothy 2:22
4 Colossians 4:6
5 1 Peter 3:2
6 Matthew 5:28
7 Ephesians 5:4
8 Ephesians 5:3
9 Romans 12:17; Proverbs 27:23
10 Leviticus 25:35; Philippians 2:4
11 1 Timothy 5:8
12 Proverbs 28:19; 21:6; Job 20:19-20
13 Zechariah 8:16
14 1 Peter 3:16
15 3 John 12
16 Proverbs 14:5, 25

Q. 78. *What is forbidden in the ninth commandment?*
A. The ninth commandment forbids whatsoever is prejudicial to truth, or injurious to our own, or our neighbour's, good name.[1]

Q. 79. *Which is the tenth commandment?*
A. The tenth commandment is, You shall not covet your neighbour's house; you shall not covet your neighbour's wife, or his male servant, or his female servant, or his ox, or his donkey, or anything that is your neighbour's.

Q. 80. *What is required in the tenth commandment?*
A. The tenth commandment requires full contentment with our own condition,[2] with a right and charitable frame of spirit toward our neighbour, and all that is his.[3]

Q. 81. *What is forbidden in the tenth commandment?*
A. The tenth commandment forbids all discontentment with our own estate,[4] envying or grieving at the good of our neighbour,[5] and all inordinate motions and affections to anything that is his.[6]

Q. 82. *Is any man able perfectly to keep the commandments of God?*
A. No mere man, since the fall, is able in this life perfectly to keep the commandments of God,[7] but does daily break them in thought,[8] word,[9] and deed.[10]

Q. 83. *Are all transgressions of the law equally heinous?*
A. Some sins in themselves, and by reason of several aggravations, are more heinous in the sight of God than others.[11]

Q. 84. *What does every sin deserve?*
A. Every sin deserves God's wrath and curse, both in this life, and that which is to come.[12]

---

1   Psalms 15:3; Job 27:5; Romans 3:13
2   Hebrews 13:5
3   Romans 12:15; 1 Corinthians 13:4–6
4   1 Corinthians 10:10
5   Galatians 5:26
6   Colossians 3:5
7   Ecclesiastes 7:20
8   Genesis 8:21
9   James 3:8
10 James 3:2
11 John 19:11
12 Galatians 3:10; Matthew 25:41

Q. 85. *What does God require of us, that we may escape his wrath and curse, due to us for sin?*

A. To escape the wrath and curse of God, due to us for sin, God requires of us faith in Jesus Christ, repentance unto life,[1] with the diligent use of all the outward means whereby Christ communicates to us the benefits of redemption.[2]

Q. 86. *What is faith in Jesus Christ?*

A. Faith in Jesus Christ is a saving grace,[3] whereby we receive[4] and rest upon him alone for salvation,[5] as he is offered to us in the gospel.[6]

Q. 87. *What is repentance unto life?*

A. Repentance unto life is a saving grace,[7] whereby a sinner, out of a true sense of his sin,[8] and apprehension of the mercy of God in Christ,[9] does, with grief and hatred of his sin, turn from it unto God,[10] with full purpose of, and endeavor after, new obedience.[11]

Q. 88. *What are the outward means whereby Christ communicates to us the benefits of redemption?*

A. The outward and ordinary means whereby Christ communicates to us the benefits of redemption are, his ordinances, especially the Word, sacraments, and prayer; all of which are made effectual to the elect for salvation.[12]

Q. 89. *How is the Word made effectual to salvation?*

A. The Spirit of God makes the reading, but especially the preaching, of the Word, an effectual means of convincing and converting sinners,[13] and of building them up in holiness and comfort,[14] through faith, unto salvation.[15]

---

1 Acts 20:21
2 Proverbs 2:1–5
3 Hebrews 10:39
4 John 1:12
5 Philippians 3:9
6 Isaiah 33:22
7 Acts 11:18
8 Acts 2:37
9 Joel 2:13
10 Jeremiah 31:18–19
11 Psalms 119:59
12 Acts 2:41–42
13 Psalm 19:7
14 1 Thessalonians 1:6
15 Romans 1:16

Q. 90. *How is the Word to be read and heard, that it may become effectual to salvation?*

A. That the Word may become effectual to salvation, we must practise the preaching and reading of the Word with diligence,[1] preparation,[2] and prayer;[3] receive it with faith[4] and love,[5] lay it up in our hearts,[6] and practise it in our lives.[7]

Q. 91. *How do the sacraments become effectual means of salvation?*

A. The sacraments become effectual means of salvation, not from any virtue in them, or in him who administers them;[8] but only by the blessing of Christ, and the working of his Spirit in them that by faith receive them.[9]

Q. 92. *What is a sacrament?*

A. A sacrament is a holy ordinance instituted by Christ;[10] wherein, by sensible signs, Christ, and the benefits of the new covenant, are represented, sealed, and applied to believers.[11]

Q. 93. *Which are the sacraments of the New Testament?*

A. The sacraments of the New Testament are, baptism,[12] and the Lord's Supper.[13]

Q. 94. *What is baptism?*

A. Baptism is a sacrament, wherein the washing with water in the name of the Father, and of the Son, and of the Holy Spirit,[14] signifies and seals our ingrafting into Christ, and partaking of the benefits of the covenant of grace,[15] and our engagement to be the Lord's.[16]

---

1   Proverbs 8:34
2   1 Peter 2:1–2
3   Psalms 119:18
4   Hebrews 4:2
5   2 Thessalonians 2:10
6   Psalm 119:11
7   James 1:25
8   1 Corinthians 3:7
9   1 Peter 3:21
10 Genesis 17:10
11 Romans 4:11
12 Mark 16:16
13 1 Corinthians 11:23–26
14 Matthew 28:19
15 Romans 6:3
16 Romans 6:4

Q. 95. *To whom is baptism to be administered?*

A. Baptism is not to be administered to any that are out of the visible church, till they profess their faith in Christ, and obedience to him;[1] but the infants of such as are members of the visible church are to be baptised.[2]

Q. 96. *What is the Lord's Supper?*

A. The Lord's Supper is a sacrament, wherein, by giving and receiving bread and wine, according to Christ's appointment, his death is showed forth;[3] and the worthy receivers are, not after a corporal and carnal manner, but by faith, made partakers of his body and blood, with all his benefits, to their spiritual nourishment, and growth in grace.[4]

Q. 97. *What is required for the worthy receiving of the Lord's Supper?*

A. It is required of those who would worthily partake of the Lord's Supper, that they examine themselves of their knowledge to discern the Lord's body,[5] of their faith to feed upon him,[6] of their repentance,[7] love,[8] and new obedience;[9] lest, coming unworthily, they eat and drink judgment to themselves.[10]

Q. 98. *What is prayer?*

A. Prayer is an offering up of our desires unto God,[11] for things agreeable to his will,[12] in the name of Christ,[13] with confession of our sins,[14] and thankful acknowledgment of his mercies.[15]

Q. 99. *What rule has God given for our direction in prayer?*

A. The whole Word of God is of use to direct us in prayer;[16] but the

---

1   Acts 2:41
2   Genesis 17:7, 10; Acts 2:38–39
3   Luke 22:19–20
4   1 Corinthians 10:16
5   1 Corinthians 11:28–29
6   2 Corinthians 13:5
7   1 Corinthians 11:31
8   1 Corinthians 11:18, 20
9   1 Corinthians 5:8
10 1 Corinthians 11:27
11 Psalms 62:8
12 Romans 8:27
13 John 16:23
14 Daniel 9:4
15 Philippians 4:6
16 1 John 5:14

special rule of direction is that form of prayer which Christ taught his disciples, commonly called the Lord's Prayer.[1]

Q. 100. *What does the preface of the Lord's Prayer teach us?*

A. The preface of the Lord's Prayer, which is, Our Father in heaven, teaches us to draw near to God with all holy reverence and confidence,[2] as children to a father,[3] able and ready to help us;[4] and that we should pray with and for others.[5]

Q. 101. *What do we pray for in the first petition?*

A. In the first petition, which is, Hallowed be your name, we pray that God would enable us, and others, to glorify him in all that whereby he makes himself known;[6] and that he would dispose all things to his own glory.[7]

Q. 102. *What do we pray for in the second petition?*

A. In the second petition, which is, Your kingdom come, we pray that Satan's kingdom may be destroyed;[8] and that the kingdom of grace may be advanced,[9] ourselves and others brought into it, and kept in it;[10] and that the kingdom of glory may be hastened.[11]

Q. 103. *What do we pray for in the third petition?*

A. In the third petition, which is, Your will be done in earth, as it is in heaven, we pray that God, by his grace, would make us able and willing to know, obey,[12] and submit to his will in all things,[13] as the angels do in heaven.[14]

Q. 104. *What do we pray for in the fourth petition?*

A. In the fourth petition, which is, Give us this day our daily bread, we

---

1   Matthew 6:9
2   Isaiah 64:9
3   Luke 11:13
4   Romans 8:15
5   Ephesians 6:18
6   Psalms 67:1–3
7   Romans 11:36
8   Psalm 68:1
9   Psalms 51:18
10 2 Thessalonians 3:1; Romans 10:1
11 Revelation 22:20
12 Psalm 119:34–36
13 Acts 21:14
14 Psalms 103:20, 22

pray that of God's free gift we may receive a competent portion of the good things of this life,[1] and enjoy his blessing with them.[2]

Q. 105. *What do we pray for in the fifth petition?*

A. In the fifth petition, which is, And forgive us our debts, as we also have forgiven our debtors, we pray that God, for Christ's sake, would freely pardon all our sins;[3] which we are the rather encouraged to ask, because by his grace we are enabled from the heart to forgive others.[4]

Q. 106. *What do we pray for in the sixth petition?*

A. In the sixth petition, which is, And lead us not into temptation, but deliver us from evil, we pray that God would either keep us from being tempted to sin,[5] or support and deliver us when we are tempted.[6]

Q. 107. *What does the conclusion of the Lord's Prayer teach us?*

A. The conclusion of the Lord's Prayer, which is, For yours is the kingdom, and the power, and the glory, forever. Amen, teaches us to take our encouragement in prayer from God only,[7] and in our prayers to praise him, ascribing kingdom, power, and glory to him;[8] and, in testimony of our desire, and assurance to be heard, we say, Amen[9]

---

1 Proverbs 30:8
2 Psalm 90:17
3 Psalms 51:1
4 Matthew 6:14
5 Matthew 26:41; Psalms 19:13
6 Psalm 51:10, 12
7 Daniel 9:18–19
8 1 Chronicles 29:11, 13
9 Revelation 22:20

The Creeds

The Apostles' Creed

I believe in God the Father Almighty, Maker of heaven and earth.

And in Jesus Christ, His only Son, our Lord; who was conceived by the Holy Spirit, born of the Virgin Mary; suffered under Pontius Pilate, was crucified, dead, and buried; He descended into hell; the third day He rose again from the dead; He ascended into heaven, and sits on the right hand of God the Father Almighty; from thence He shall come to judge the living and the dead.

I believe in the Holy Spirit; the holy catholic church, the communion of saints; the forgiveness of sins; the resurrection of the body; and the life everlasting. Amen.

The Nicene Creed (AD 381)

I believe in one God, the Father Almighty, Maker of heaven and earth, and of all things visible and invisible.

And in one Lord Jesus Christ, the only-begotten Son of God, begotten of the Father before all worlds; God of God, Light of Light, very God of very God; begotten, not made, being of one substance with the Father, by whom all things were made.

Who, for us men and for our salvation, came down from heaven, and was incarnate by the Holy Spirit of the virgin Mary, and was made man; and was crucified also for us under Pontius Pilate; He suffered and was buried; and the third day He rose again, according to the Scriptures; and ascended into heaven, and sits on the right hand of the Father; and He shall come again, with glory, to judge the living and the dead; whose kingdom shall have no end.

And I believe in the Holy Spirit, the Lord and Giver of Life; who proceeds from the Father and the Son; who with the Father and the Son together is worshiped and glorified; who spoke by the prophets.

And I believe in one holy catholic and apostolic Church. I acknowledge one baptism for the remission of sins; and I look for the resurrection of the dead, and the life of the world to come. Amen.

The Athanasian Creed

Whoever will be saved, before all things it is necessary that he hold the catholic faith. Which faith except every one do keep whole and undefiled, without doubt he shall perish everlastingly.

And the catholic faith is this, that we worship one God in Trinity, and Trinity in Unity; neither confounding the Persons, nor dividing the Substance. For there is one Person of the Father, another of the Son, and another of the Holy Spirit. But the Godhead of the Father, of the Son, and of the Holy Spirit is all one: the glory equal, the majesty coeternal. Such as the Father is, such is the Son, and such is the Holy Spirit. The Father uncreated, the Son uncreated, and the Holy Spirit uncreated. The Father incomprehensible, the Son incomprehensible, and the Holy Spirit incomprehensible. The Father eternal, the Son eternal, and the Holy Spirit eternal. And yet they are not three Eternals, but one Eternal. As there are not three Uncreated nor three Incomprehensibles, but one Uncreated and one Incomprehensible. So likewise the Father is almighty, the Son almighty, and the Holy Spirit almighty. And yet they are not three Almighties, but one Almighty. So the Father is God, the Son is God, and the Holy Spirit is God. And yet they are not three Gods, but one God. So likewise the Father is Lord, the Son Lord, and the Holy Spirit Lord. And yet not three Lords, but one Lord. For like as we are compelled by the Christian verity to acknowledge every Person by Himself to be God and Lord, So are we forbidden by the catholic religion to say, There be three Gods, or three Lords.

The Father is made of none: neither created nor begotten. The Son is of the Father alone; not made, nor created, but begotten. The Holy Spirit is of the Father and of the Son: neither made, nor created, nor begotten, but proceeding. So there is one Father, not three Fathers;

one Son, not three Sons; one Holy Spirit, not three Holy Spirits. And in this Trinity none is before or after other; none is greater or less than another; But the whole three Persons are coeternal together, and coequal: so that in all things, as is aforesaid, the Unity in Trinity and the Trinity in Unity is to be worshipped. He, therefore, that will be saved must thus think of the Trinity.

Furthermore, it is necessary to everlasting salvation that he also believe faithfully the incarnation of our Lord Jesus Christ. For the right faith is, that we believe and confess that our Lord Jesus Christ, the Son of God, is God and Man; God of the Substance of the Father, begotten before the worlds; and Man of the substance of His mother, born in the world; Perfect God and perfect Man, of a reasonable soul and human flesh subsisting. Equal to the Father as touching His Godhead, and inferior to the Father as touching His manhood; Who, although He be God and Man, yet He is not two, but one Christ: One, not by conversion of the Godhead into flesh, but by taking the manhood into God; One altogether; not by confusion of Substance, but by unity of Person. For as the reasonable soul and flesh is one man, so God and Man is one Christ; Who suffered for our salvation; descended into hell, rose again the third day from the dead; He ascended into heaven; He sits on the right hand of the Father, God Almighty; from whence He shall come to judge the living and the dead. At whose coming all men shall rise again with their bodies, and shall give an account of their own works. And they that have done good shall go into life everlasting; and they that have done evil, into everlasting fire.

This is the catholic faith; which except a man believe faithfully and firmly, he cannot be saved.

The Definition of the Council of Chalcedon (AD 451)

Therefore, following the holy fathers, we all with one accord teach men to acknowledge one and the same Son, our Lord Jesus Christ, at once complete in Godhead and complete in manhood, truly God and truly man, consisting also of a reasonable soul and body; of one substance with the Father as regards his Godhead, and at the same time of one substance with us as regards his manhood; like us in all respects, apart from sin; as regards his Godhead, begotten of the Father before the ages, but yet as regards his manhood begotten, for us men and for our salvation, of Mary the Virgin, the God-bearer; one and the same Christ, Son, Lord, Only-begotten, recognized in two natures, without confusion, without change, without division, without separation; the distinction of natures being in no way annulled by the union, but rather the characteristics of each nature being preserved and coming together to form one person and subsistence, not as parted or separated into two persons, but one and the same Son and Only-begotten God the Word, Lord Jesus Christ; even as the prophets from earliest times spoke of him, and our Lord Jesus Christ himself taught us, and the creed of the fathers has handed down to us.